ZEN MANDALA
COLORING BOOK FOR ADULTS

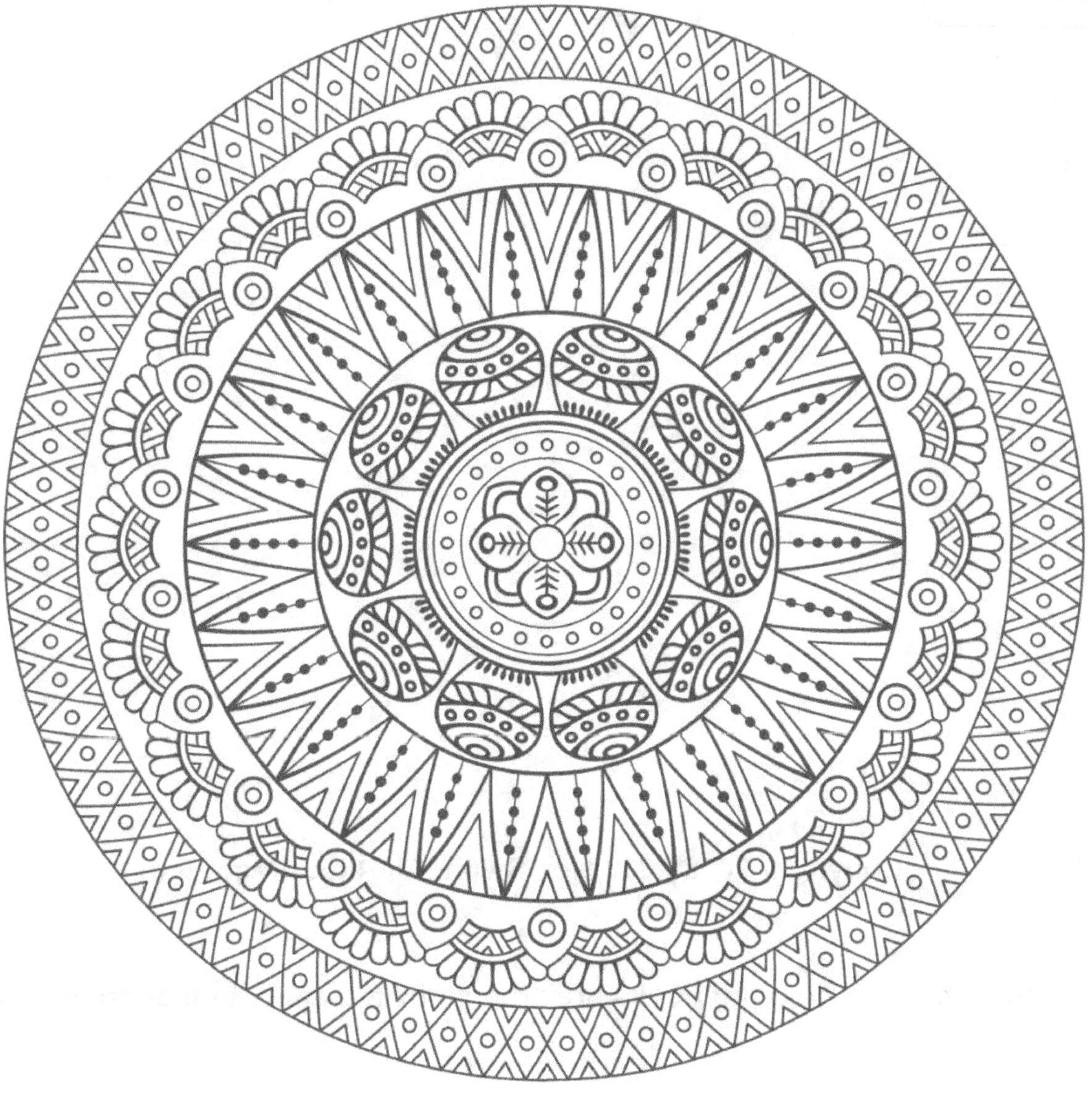

NOX SMITH

Nox Switch brand coloring books are created by a team of independent artists.

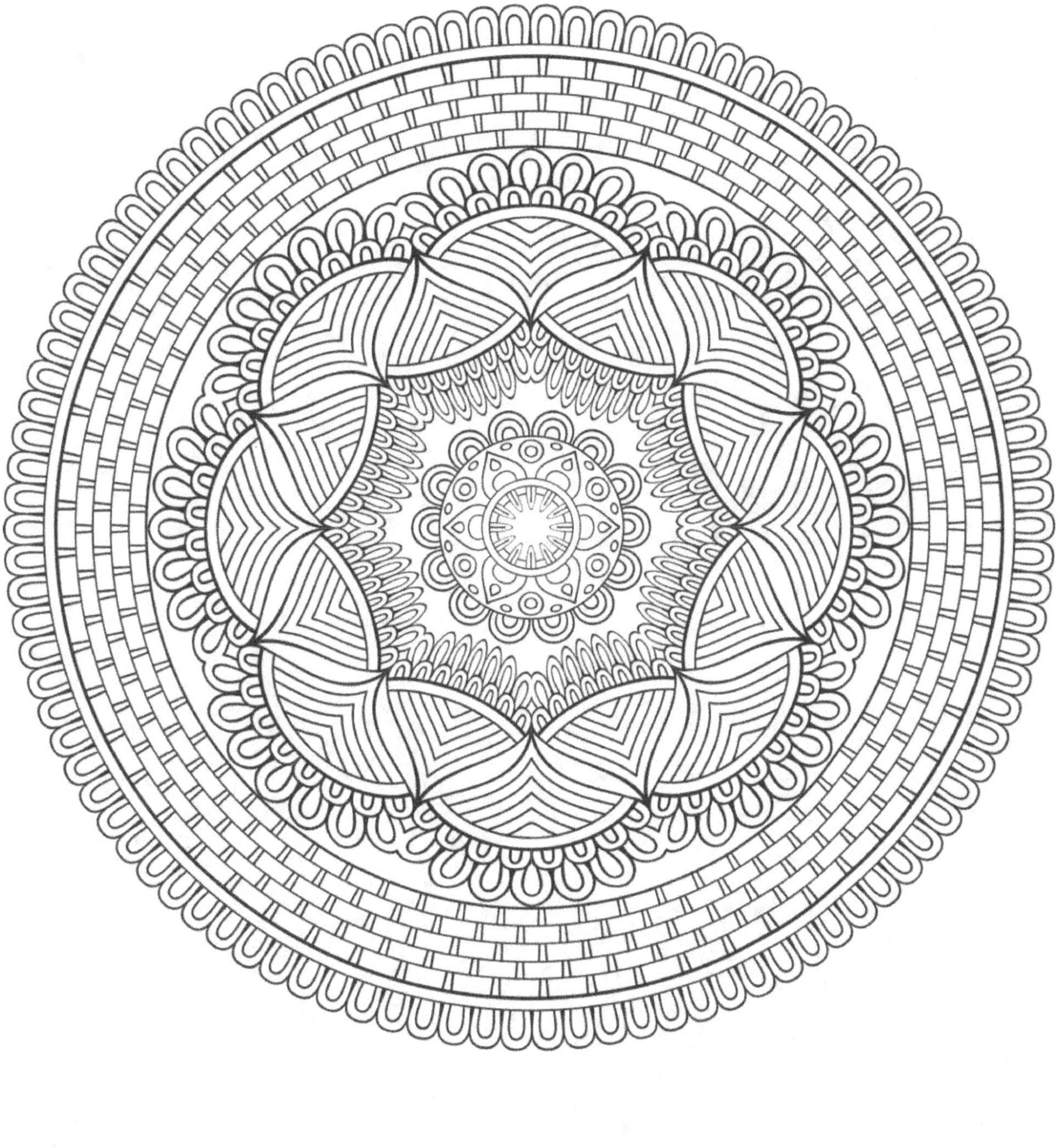

THIS BOOK BELONG TO

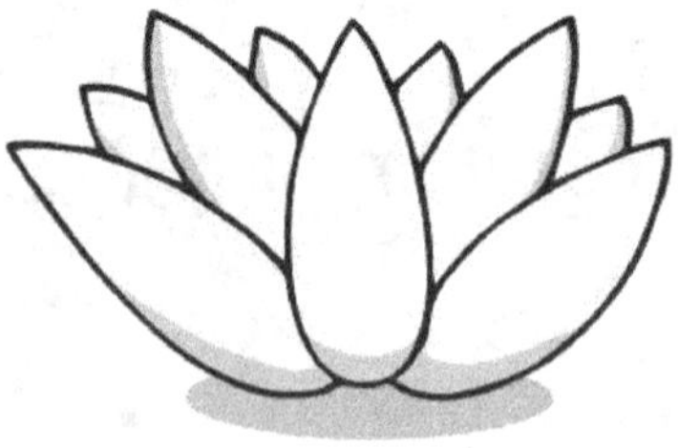

“Do not let the behavior of others destroy your inner peace.”

Dalai Lama

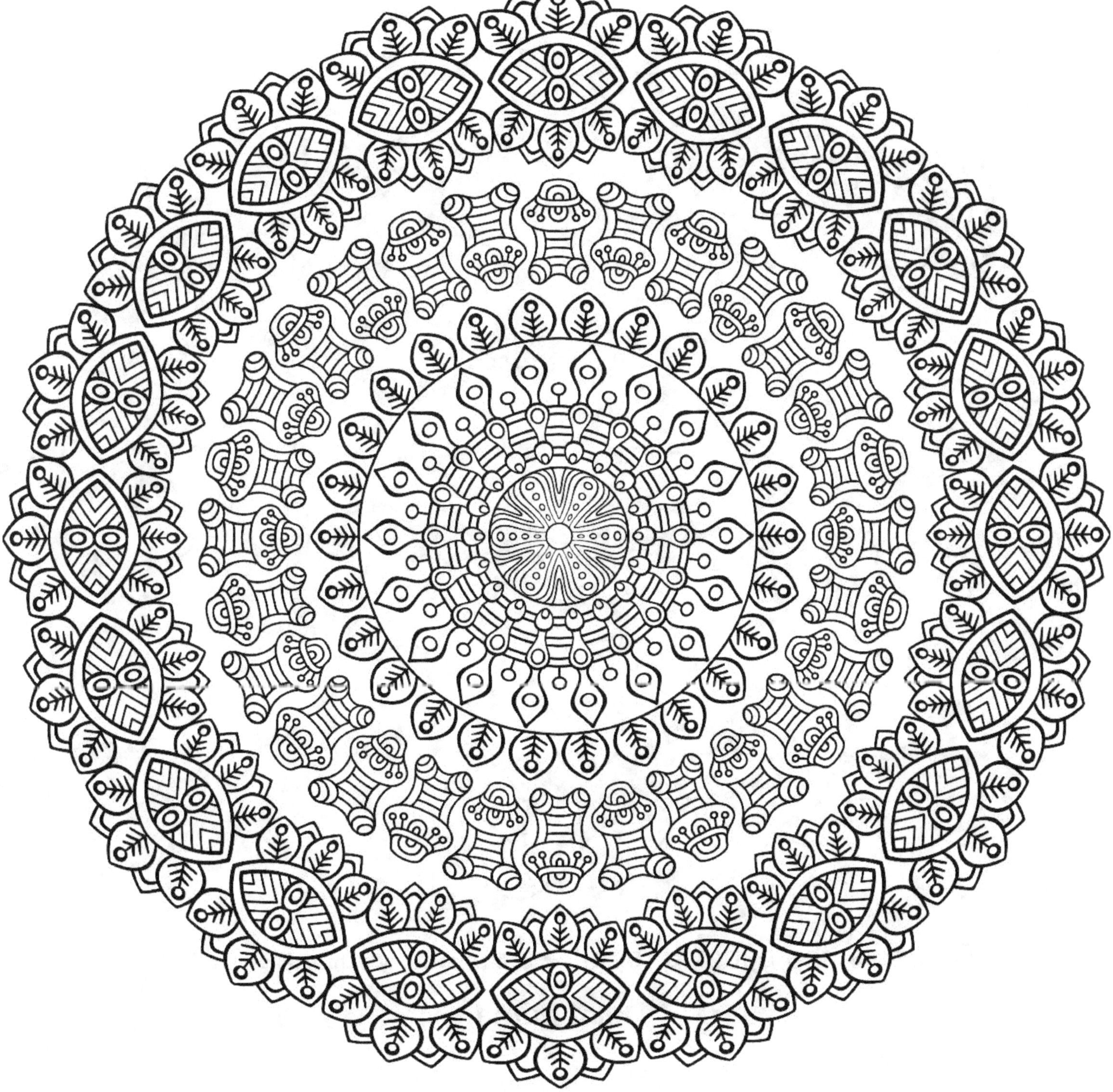

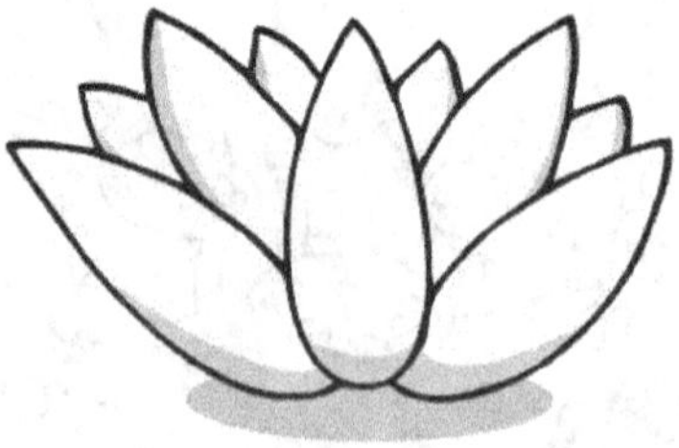

“Do not let the behavior of others destroy your inner peace.”

Dalai Lama

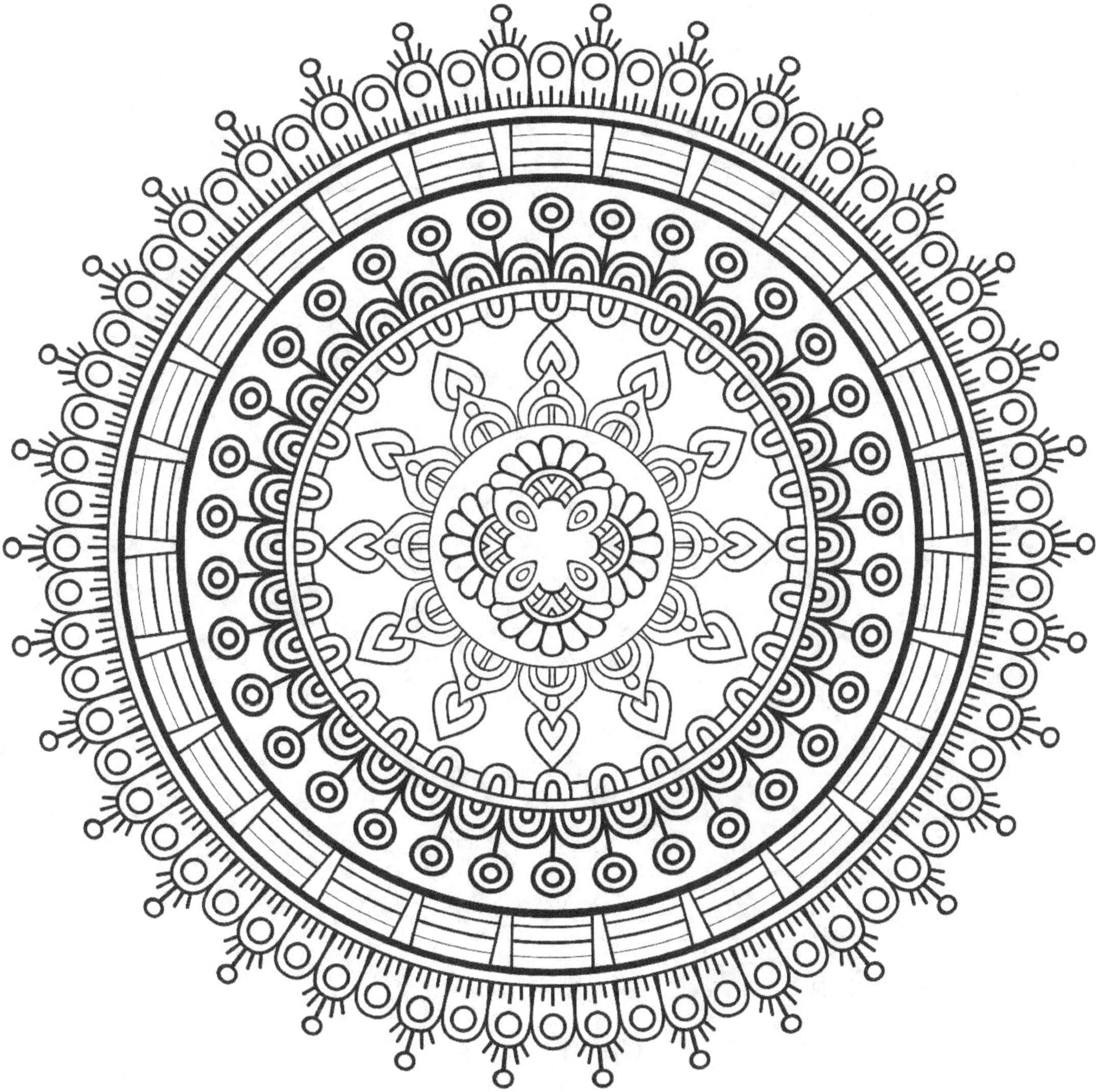

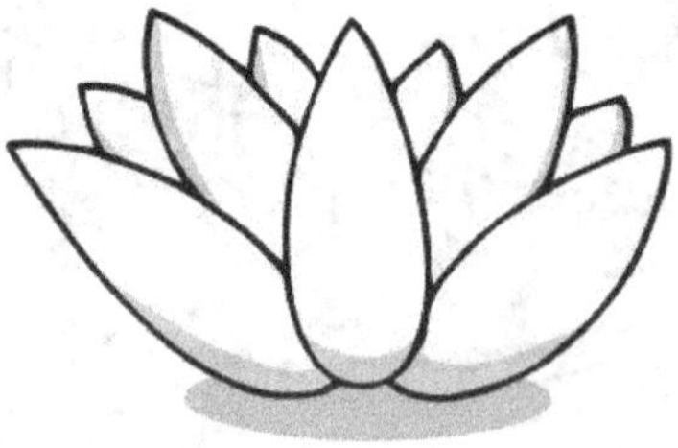

“Do not let the behavior of others destroy your inner peace.”

Dalai Lama

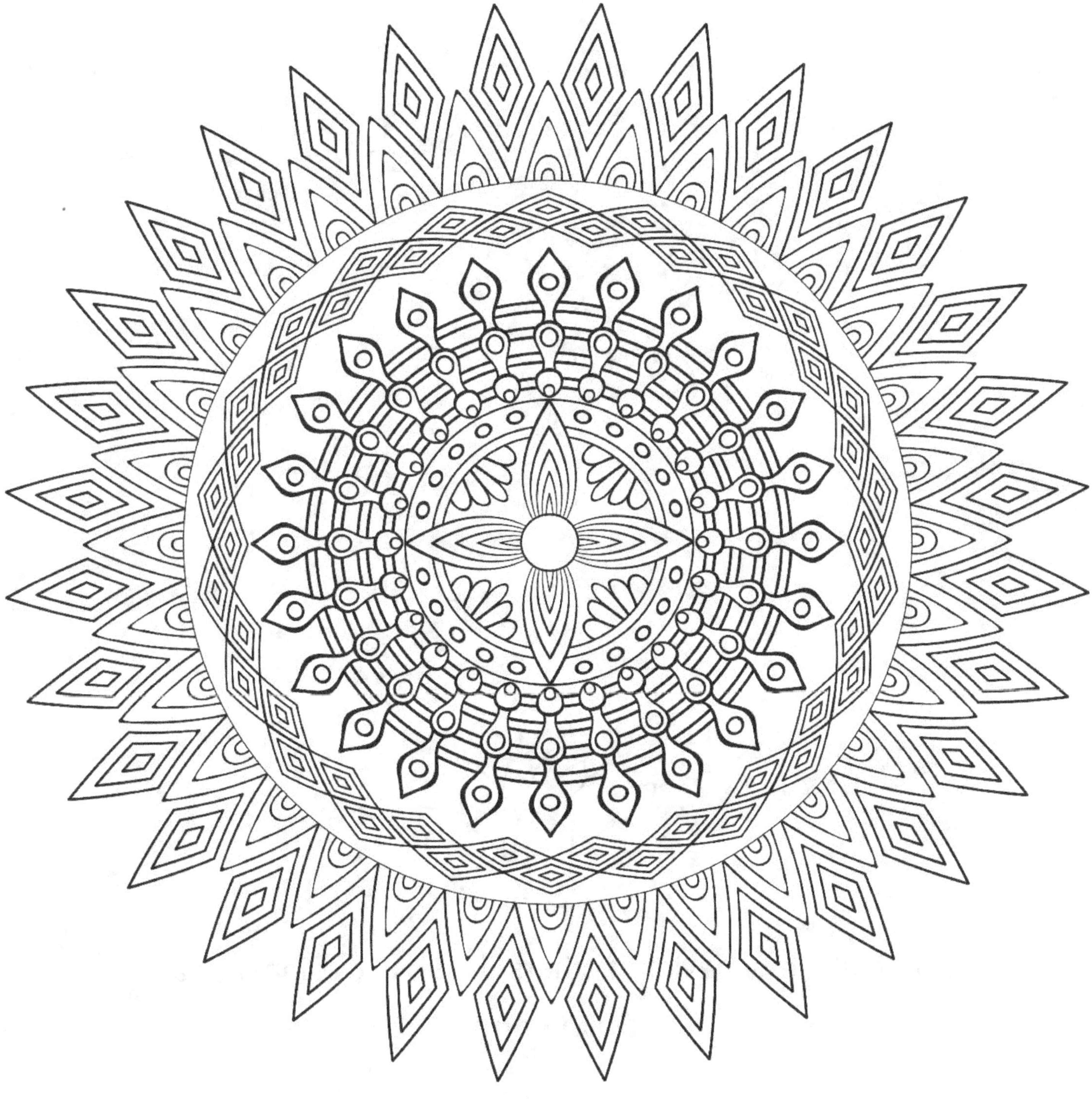

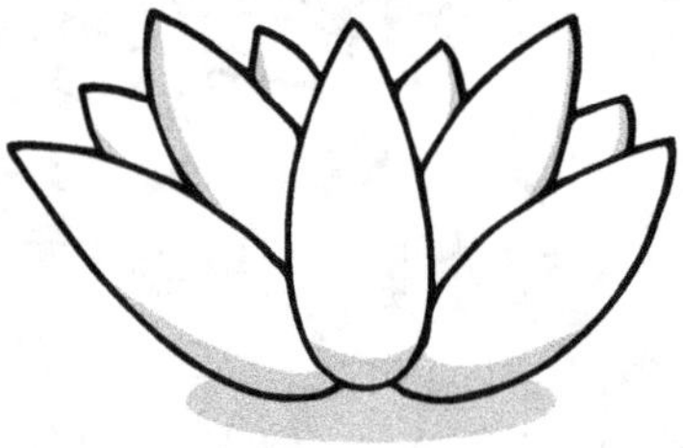

“Do not let the behavior of others destroy your inner peace.”

Dalai Lama

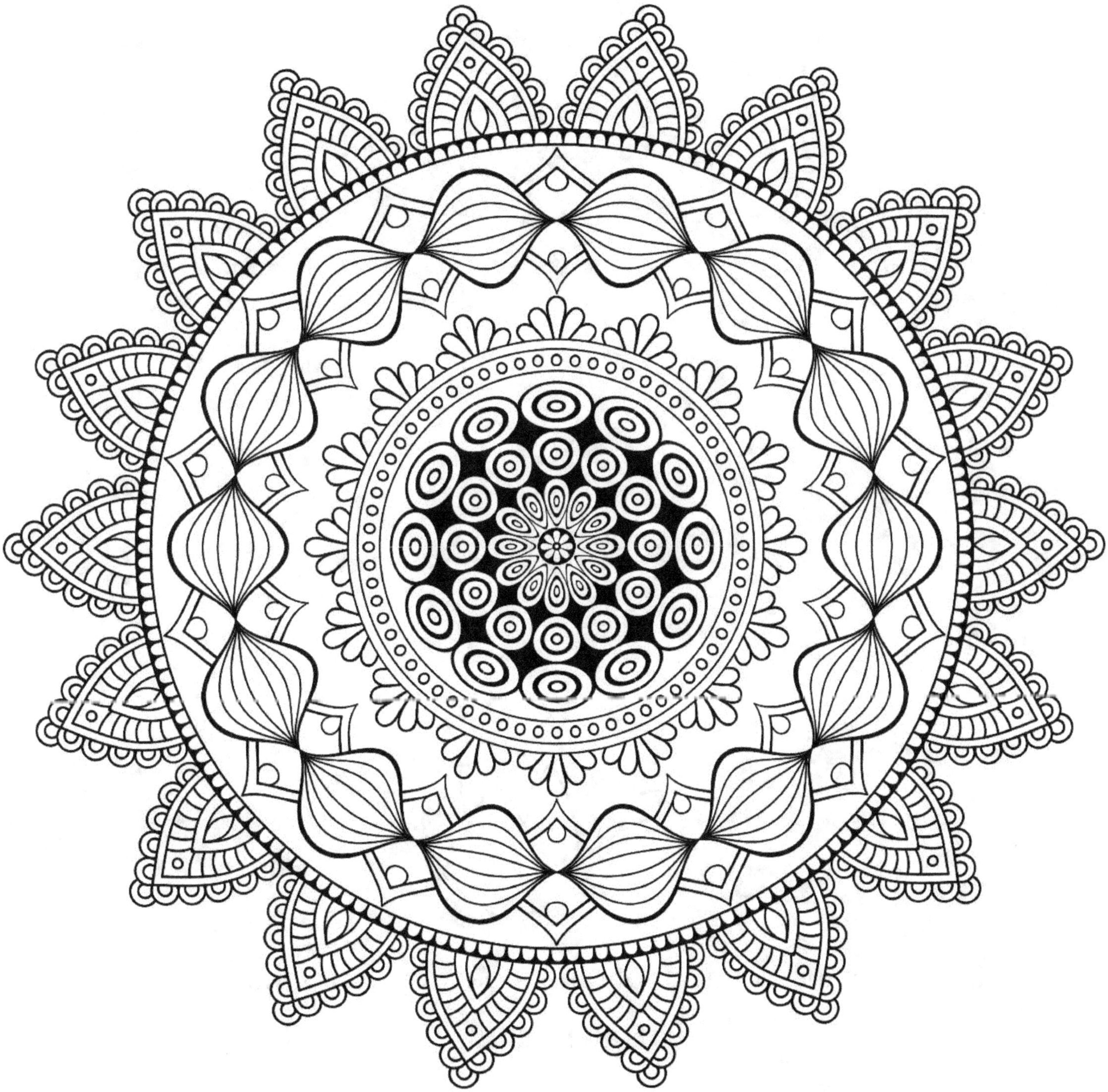

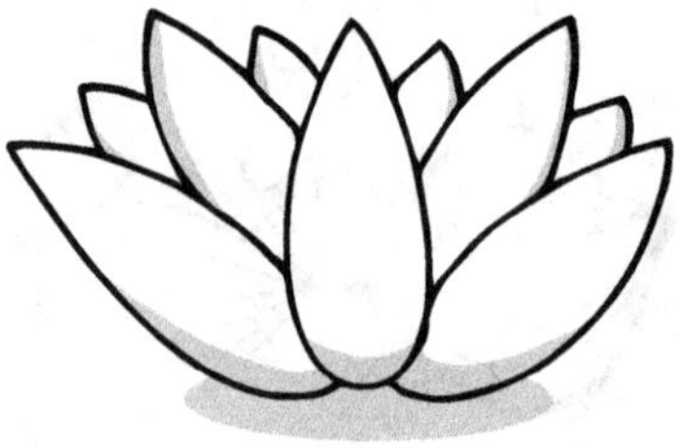

“Do not let the behavior of others destroy your inner peace.”

Dalai Lama

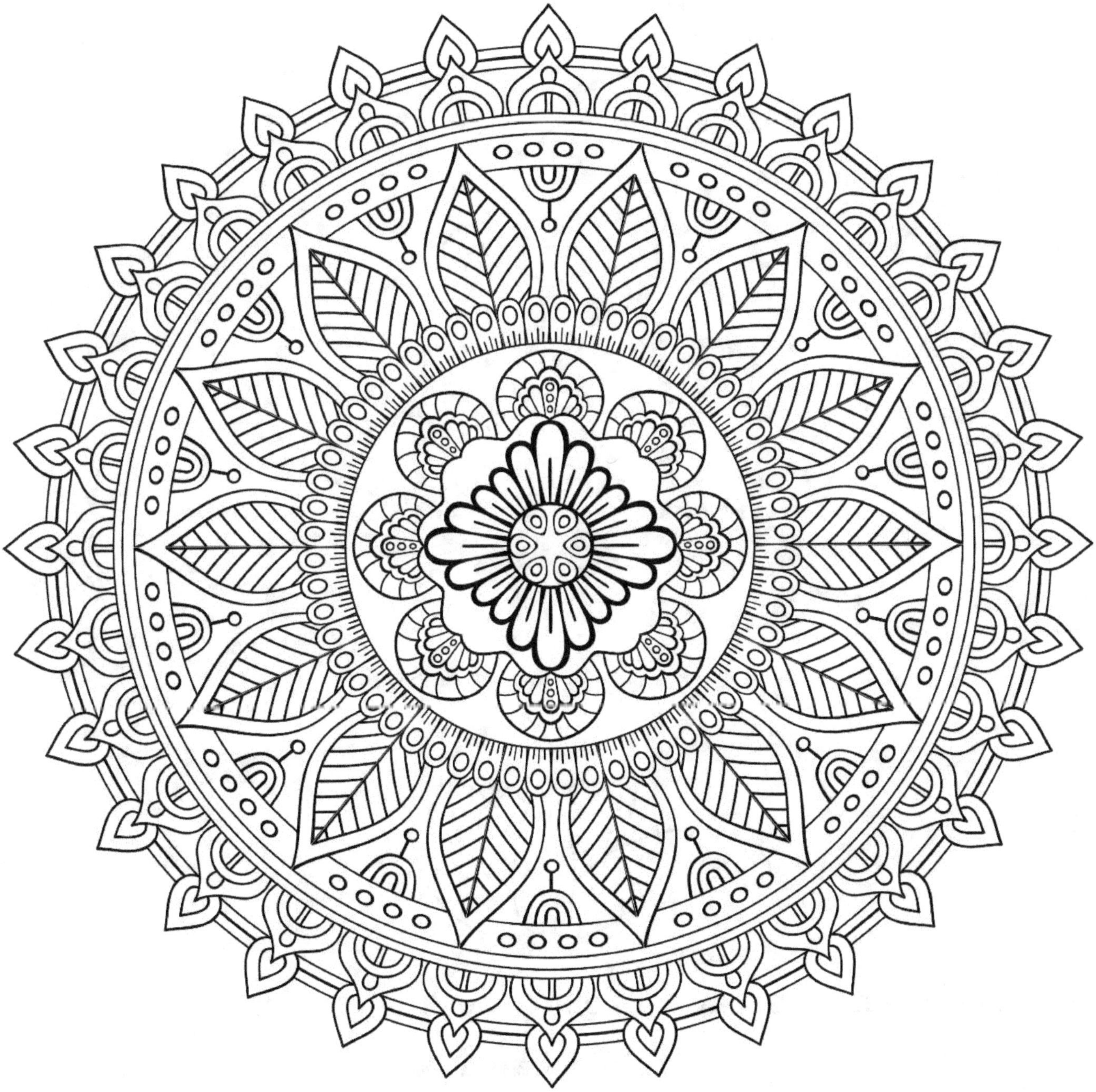

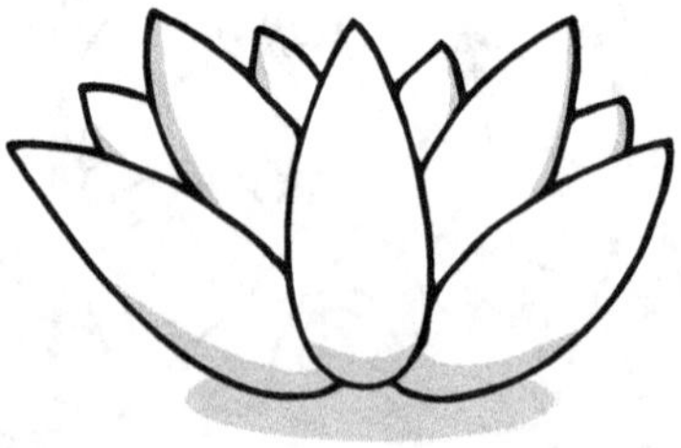

"Do not let the behavior of others destroy your inner peace."

Dalai Lama

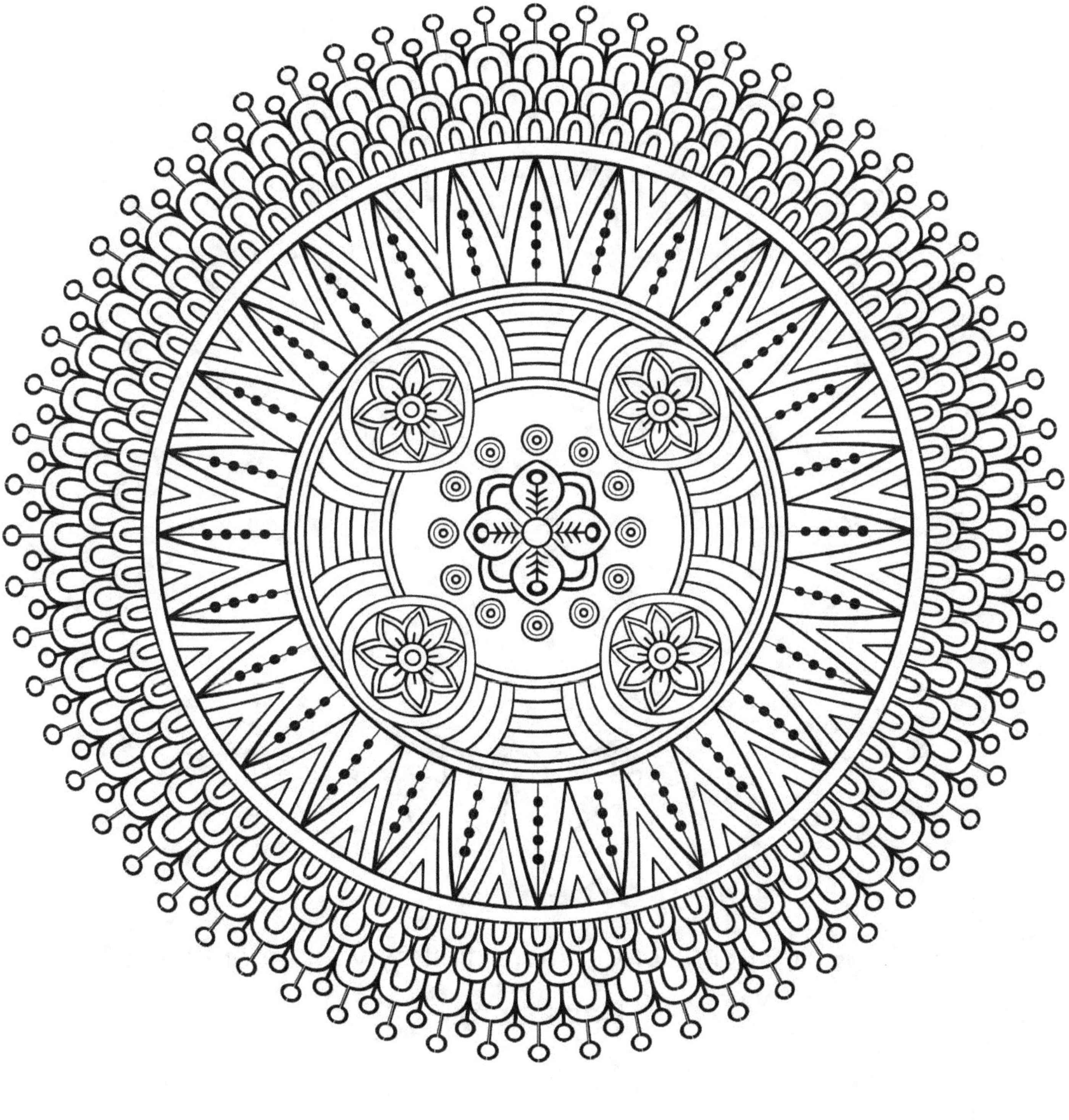

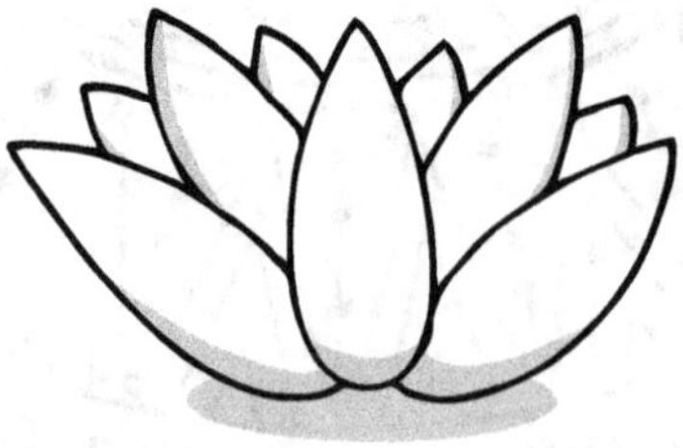

"Do not let the behavior of others destroy your inner peace."

Dalai Lama

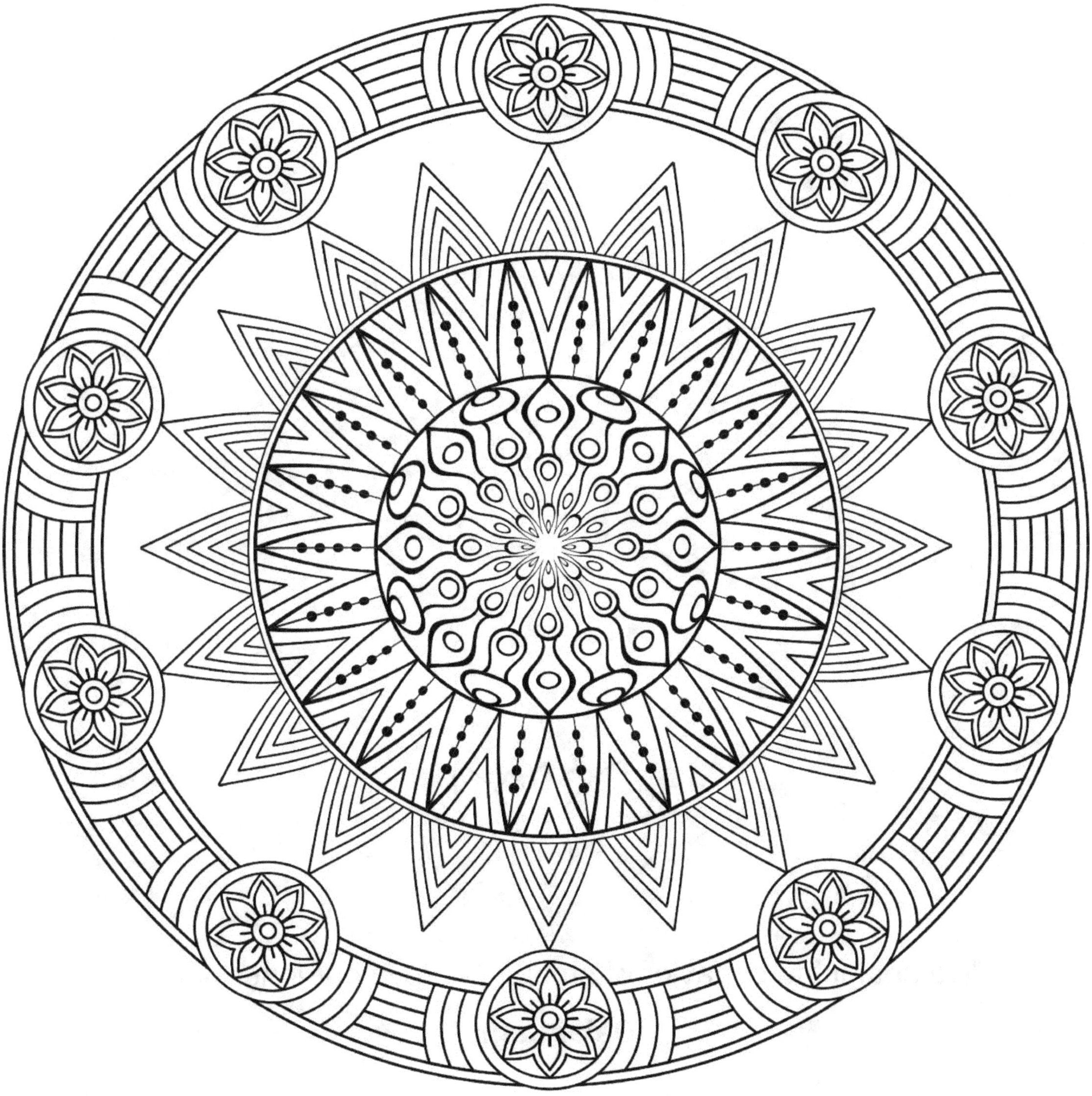

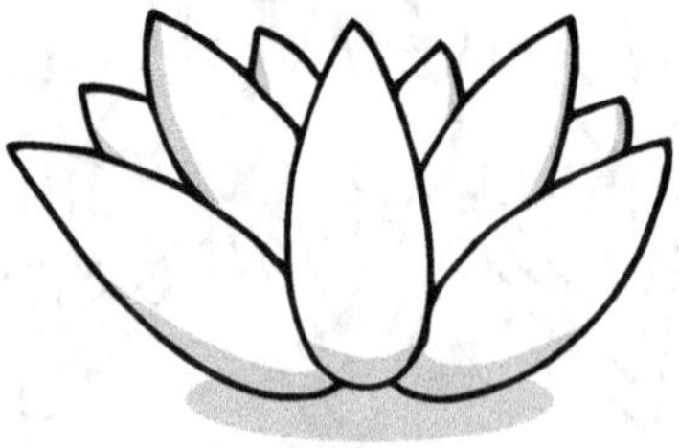

"Do not let the behavior of others destroy your inner peace."

Dalai Lama

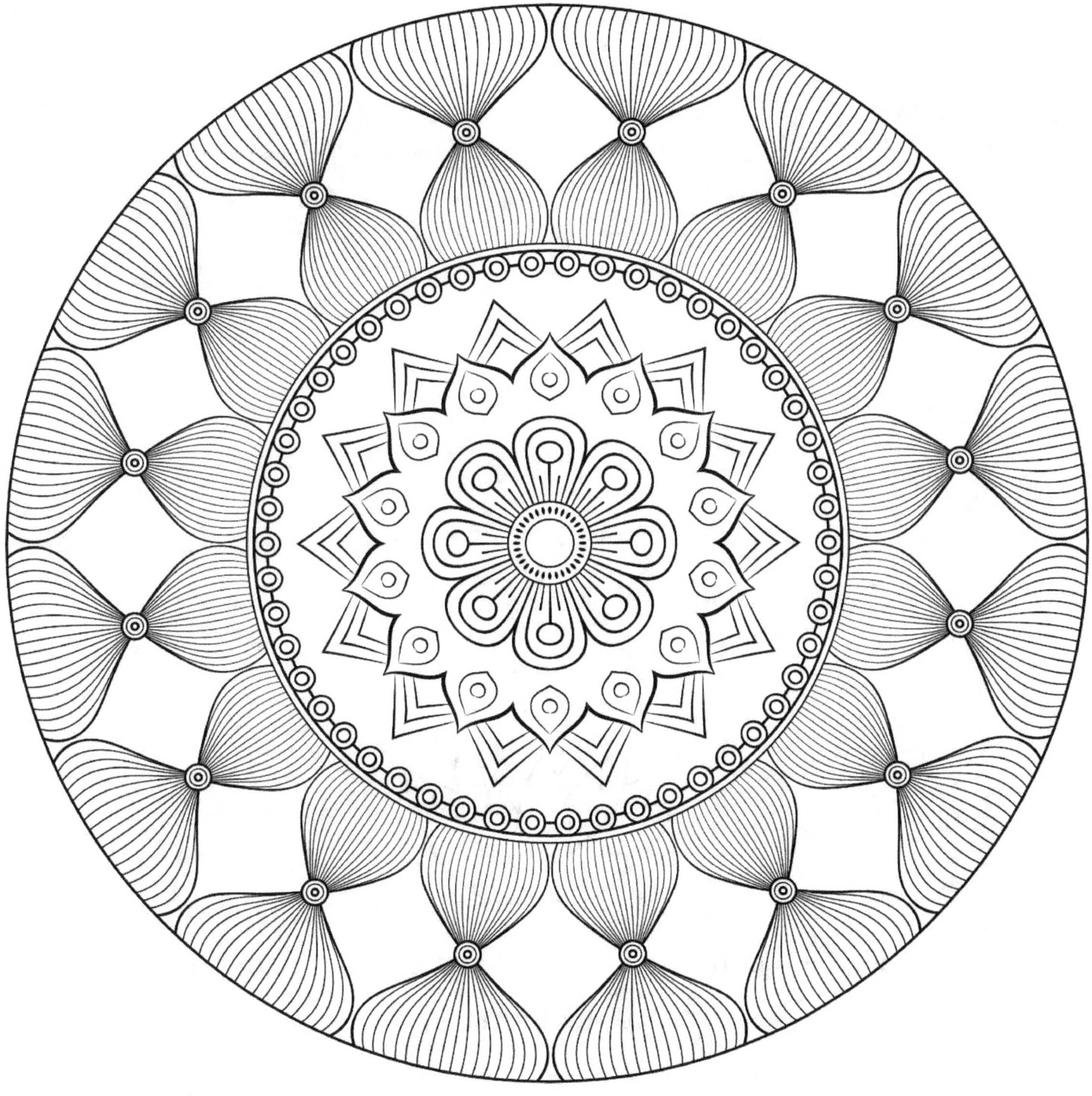

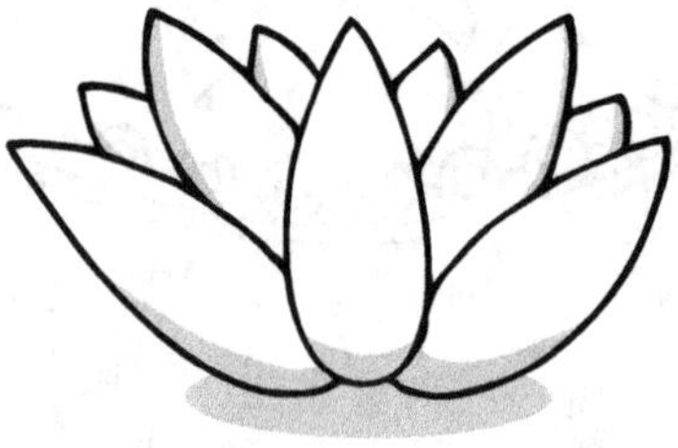

“Do not let the behavior of others destroy your inner peace.”

Dalai Lama

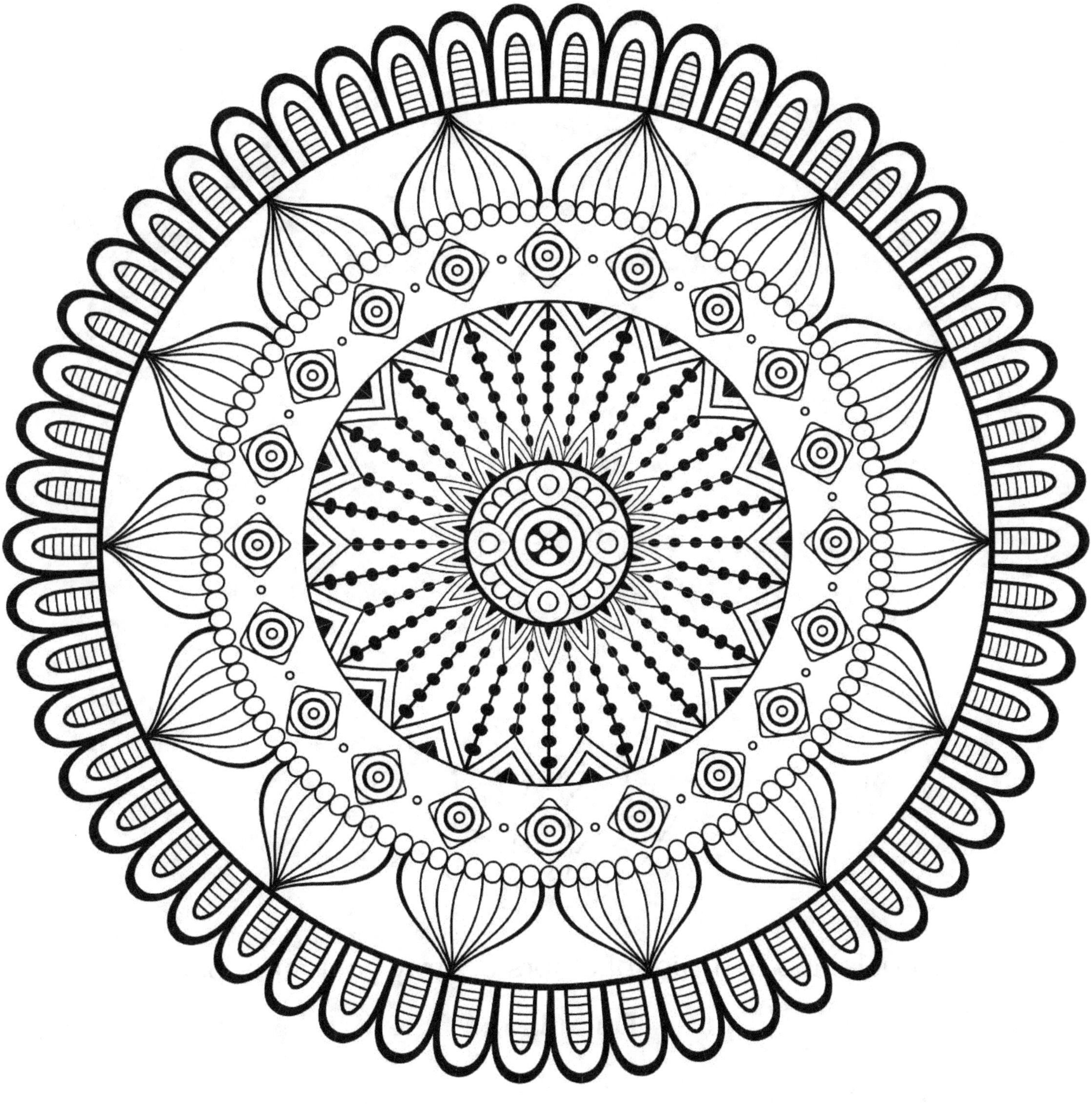

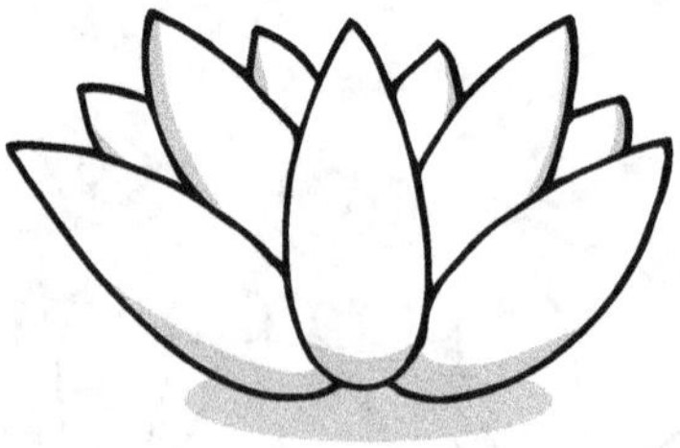

"Do not let the behavior of others destroy your inner peace."

Dalai Lama

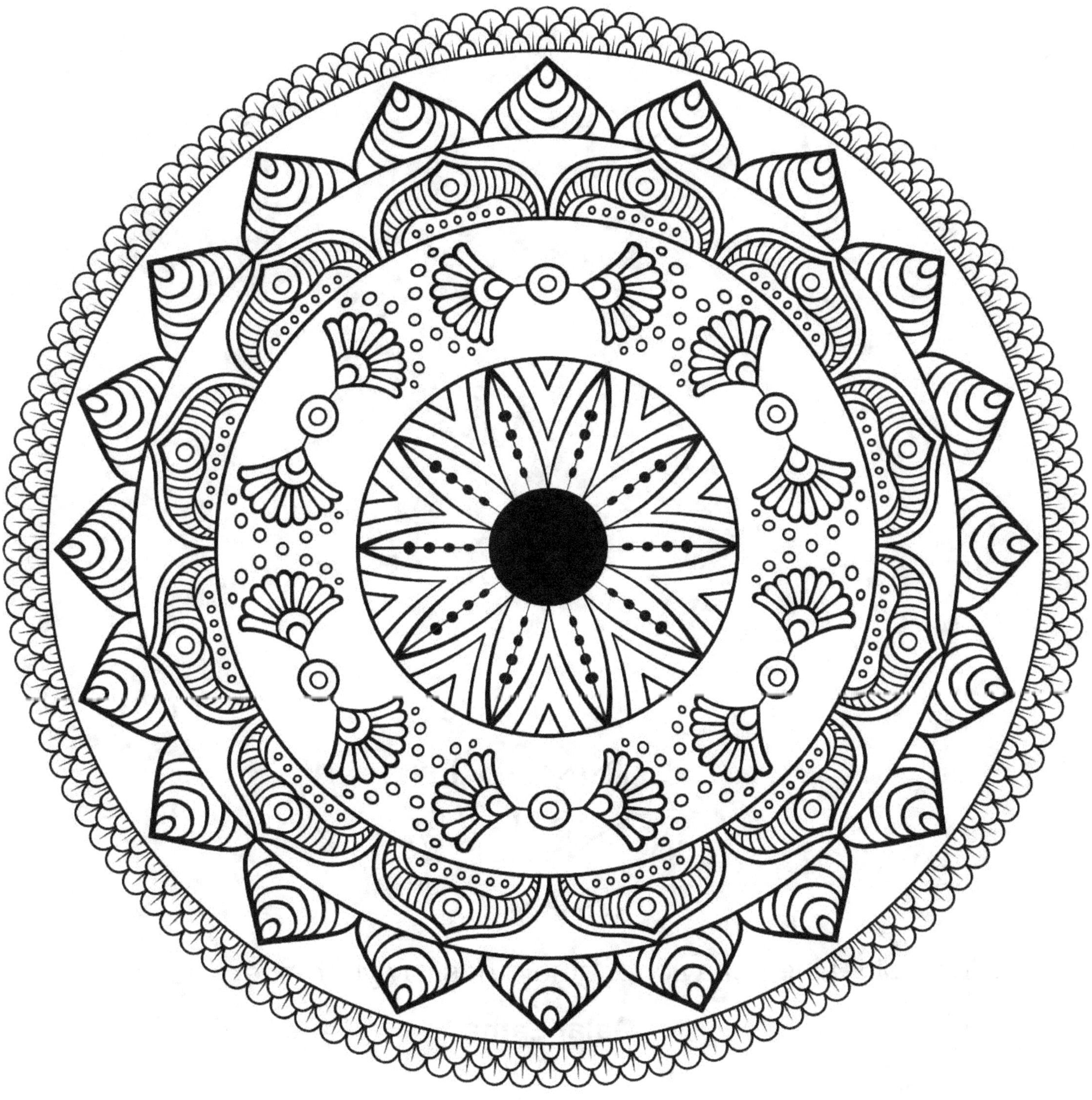

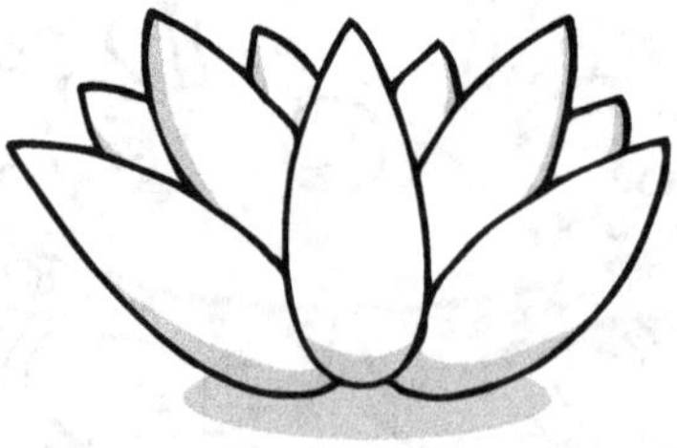

“Do not let the behavior of others destroy your inner peace.”

Dalai Lama

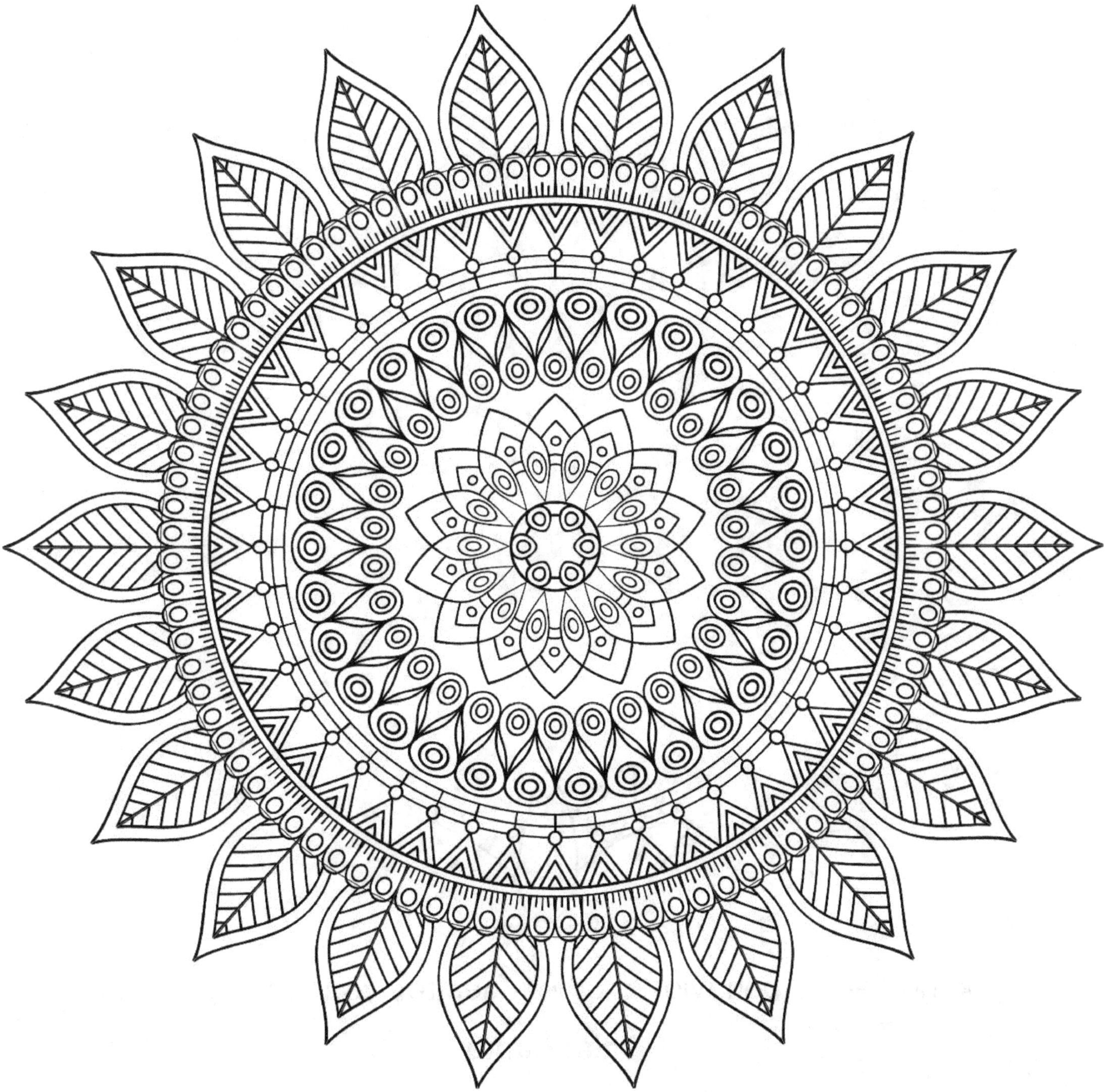

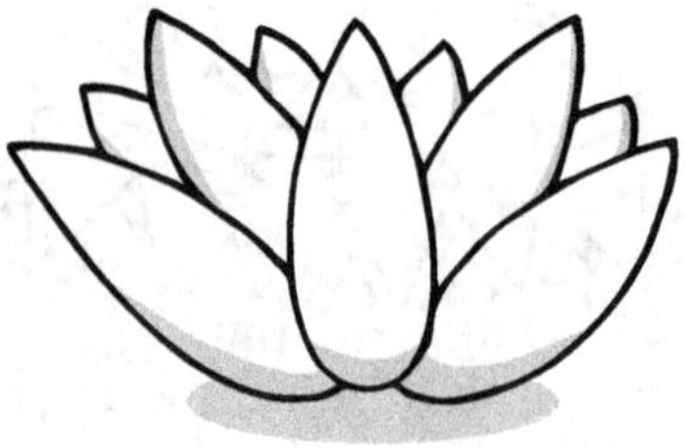

“Do not let the behavior of others destroy your inner peace.”

Dalai Lama

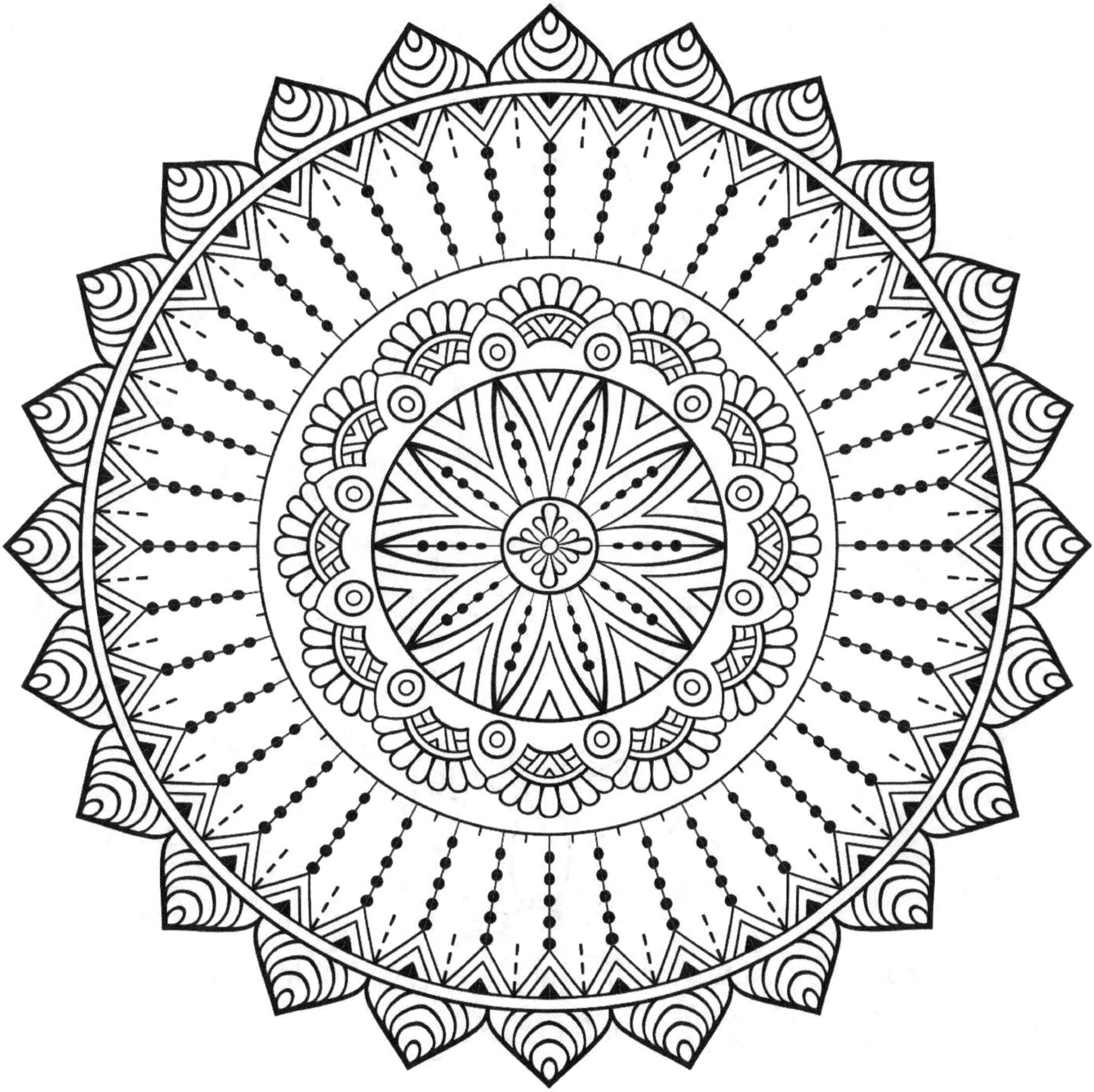

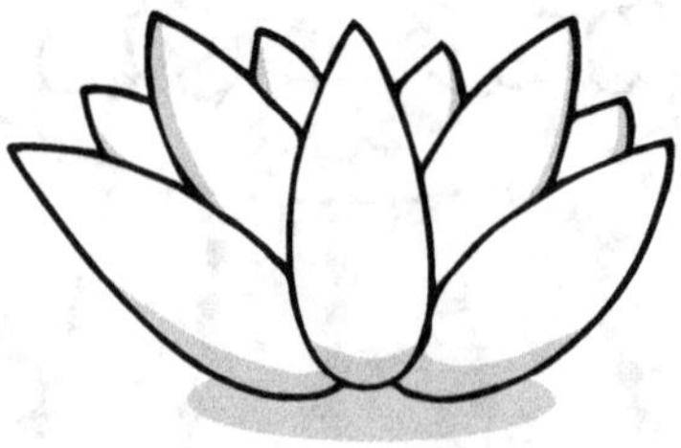

"Do not let the behavior of others destroy your inner peace."

Dalai Lama

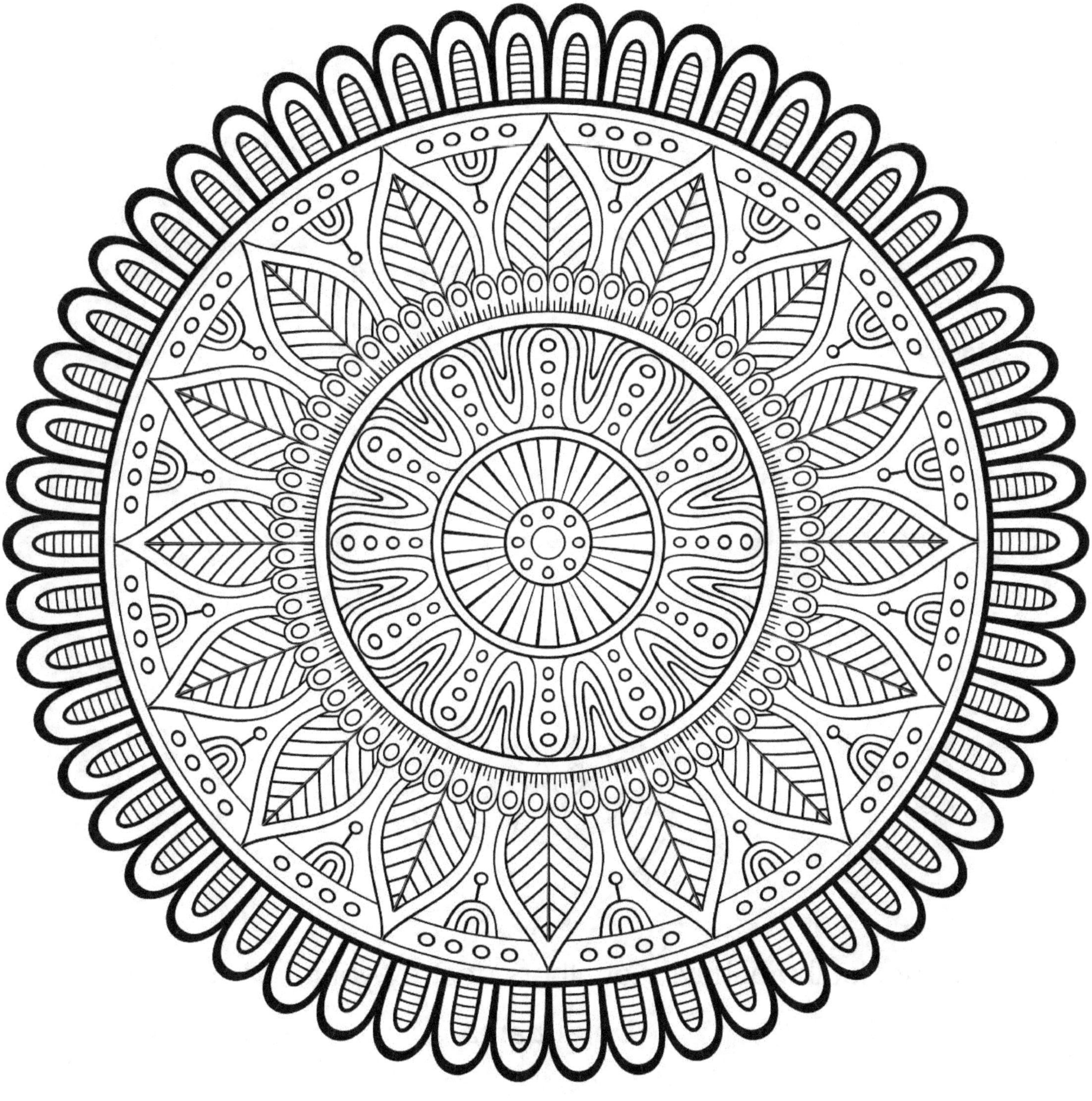

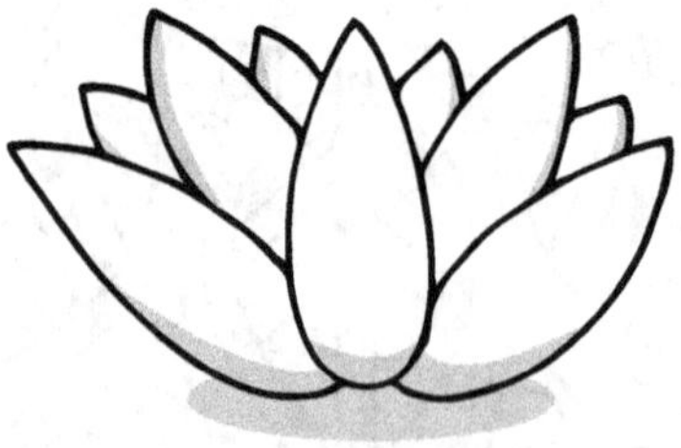

"Do not let the behavior of others destroy your inner peace."

Dalai Lama

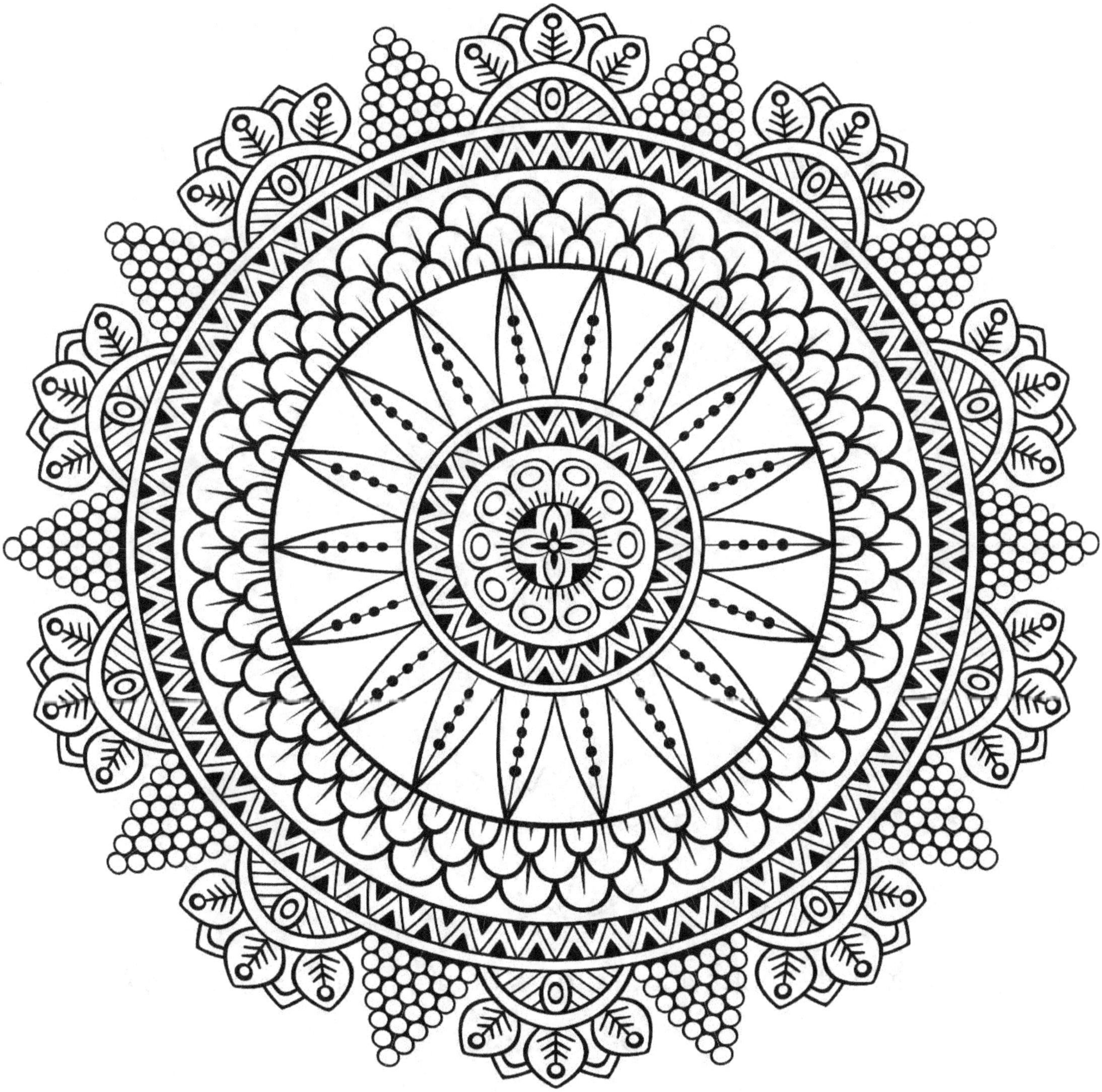

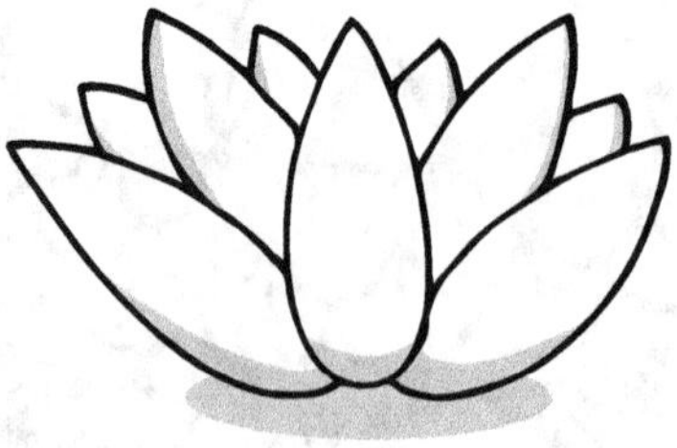

“Do not let the behavior of others destroy your inner peace.”

Dalai Lama

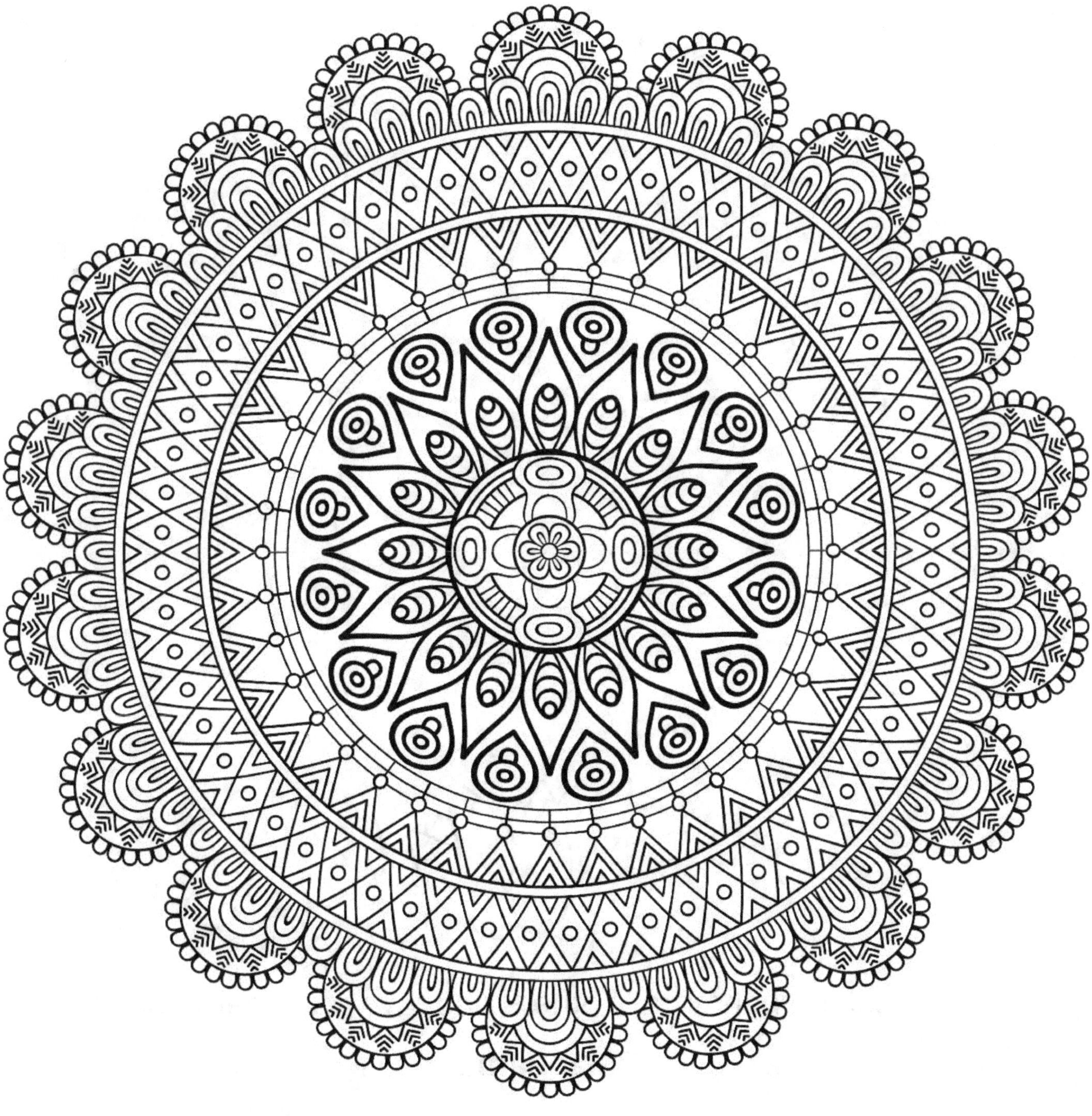

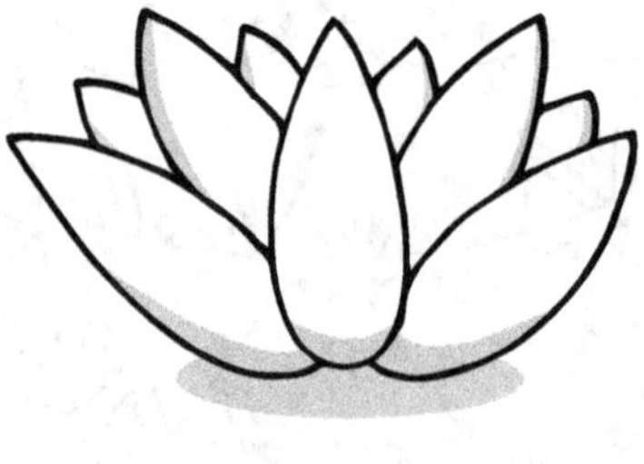

"Do not let the behavior of others destroy your inner peace."

Dalai Lama

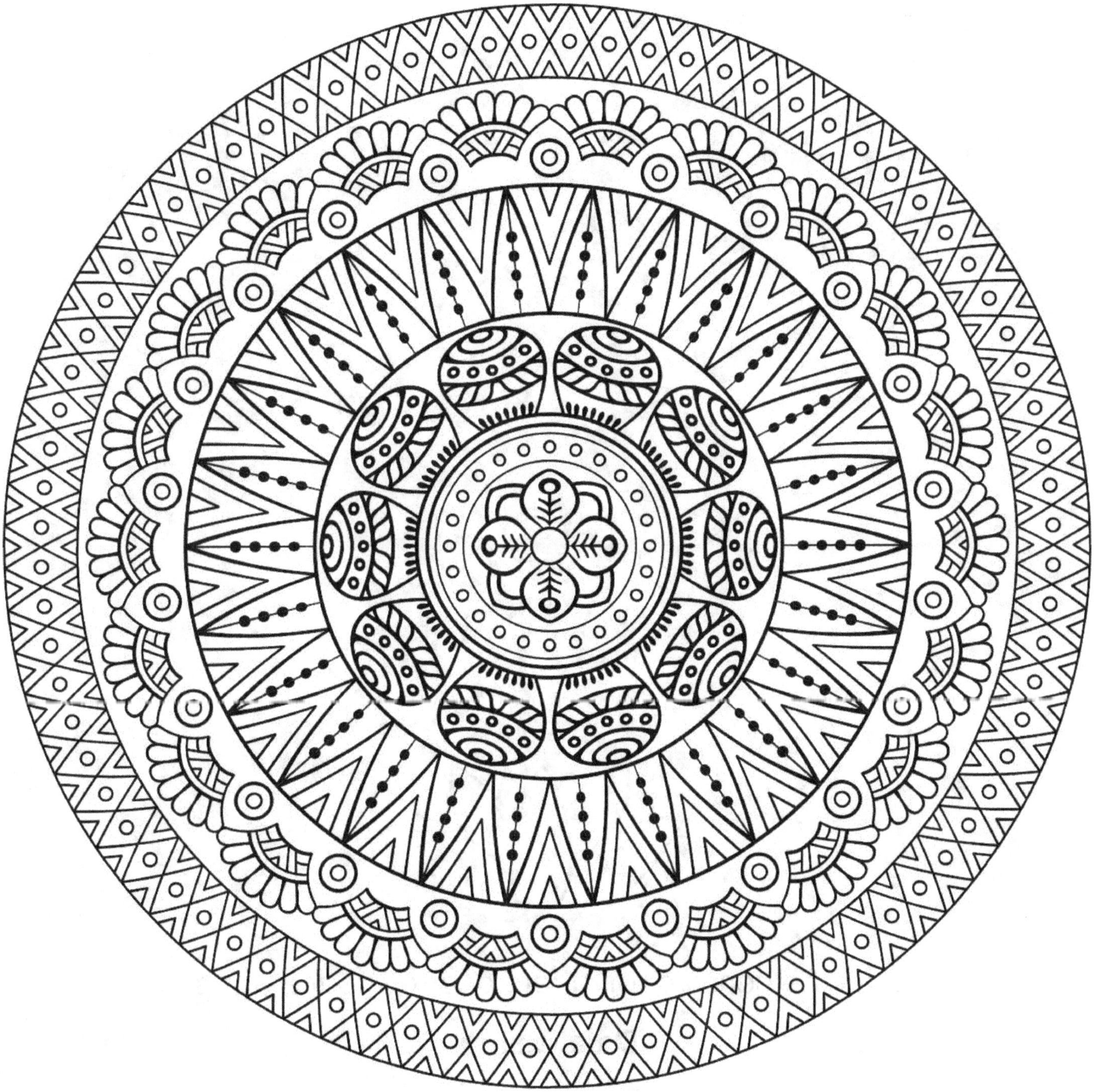

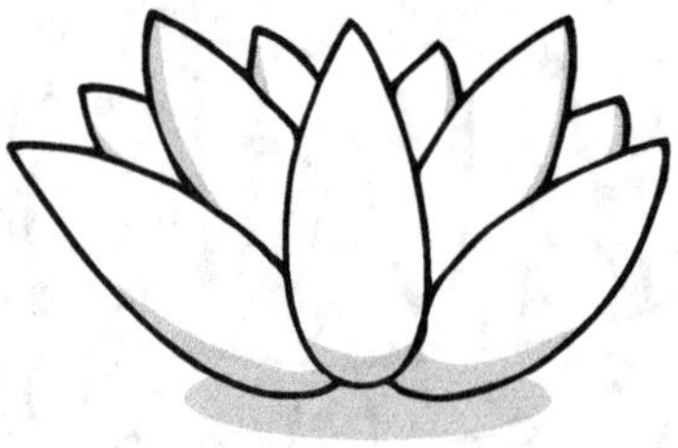

“Do not let the behavior of others destroy your inner peace.”

Dalai Lama

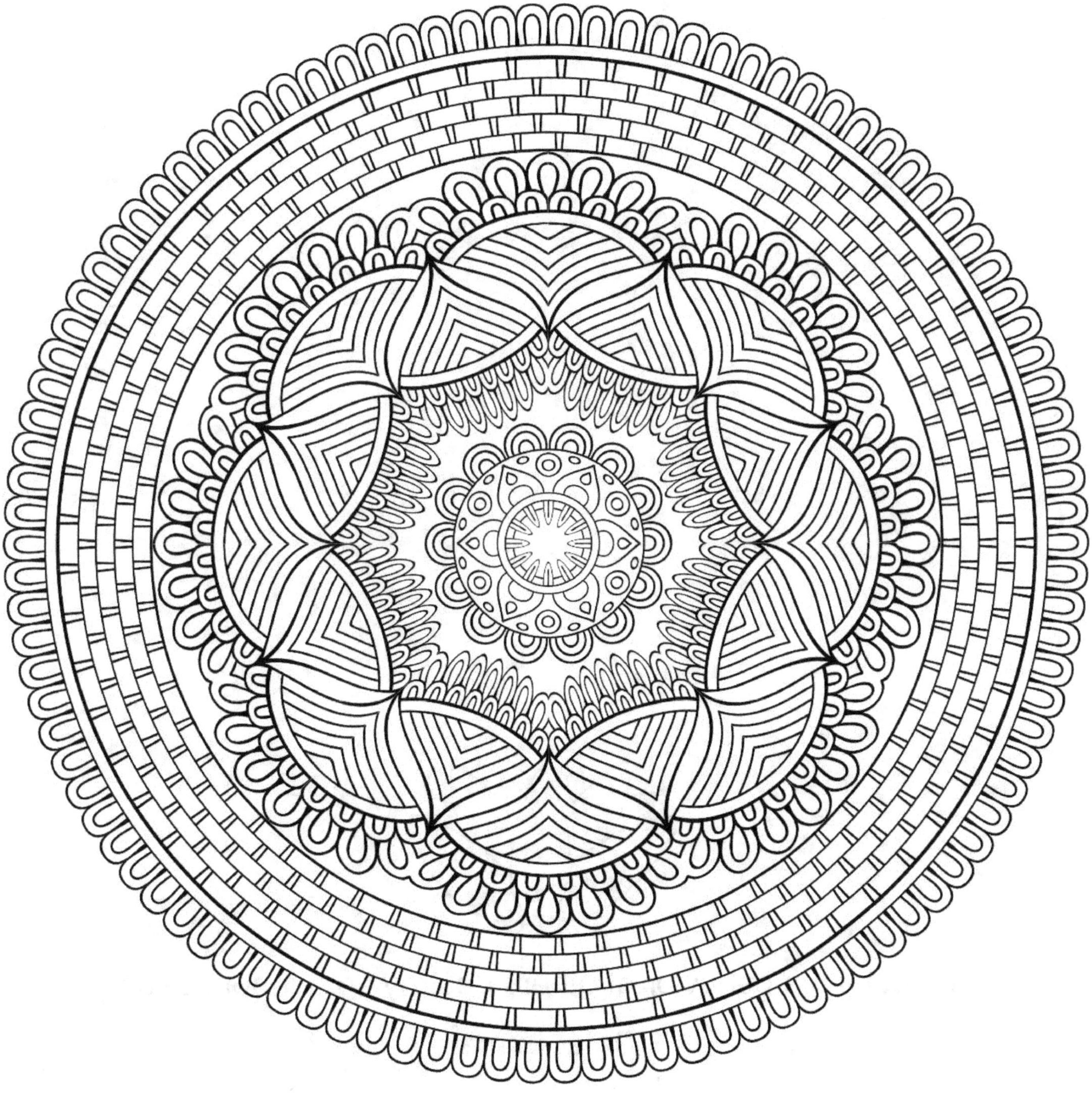

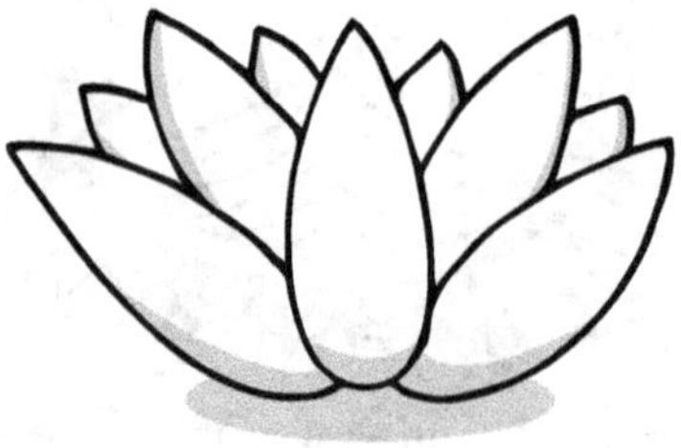

"Do not let the behavior of others destroy your inner peace."

Dalai Lama

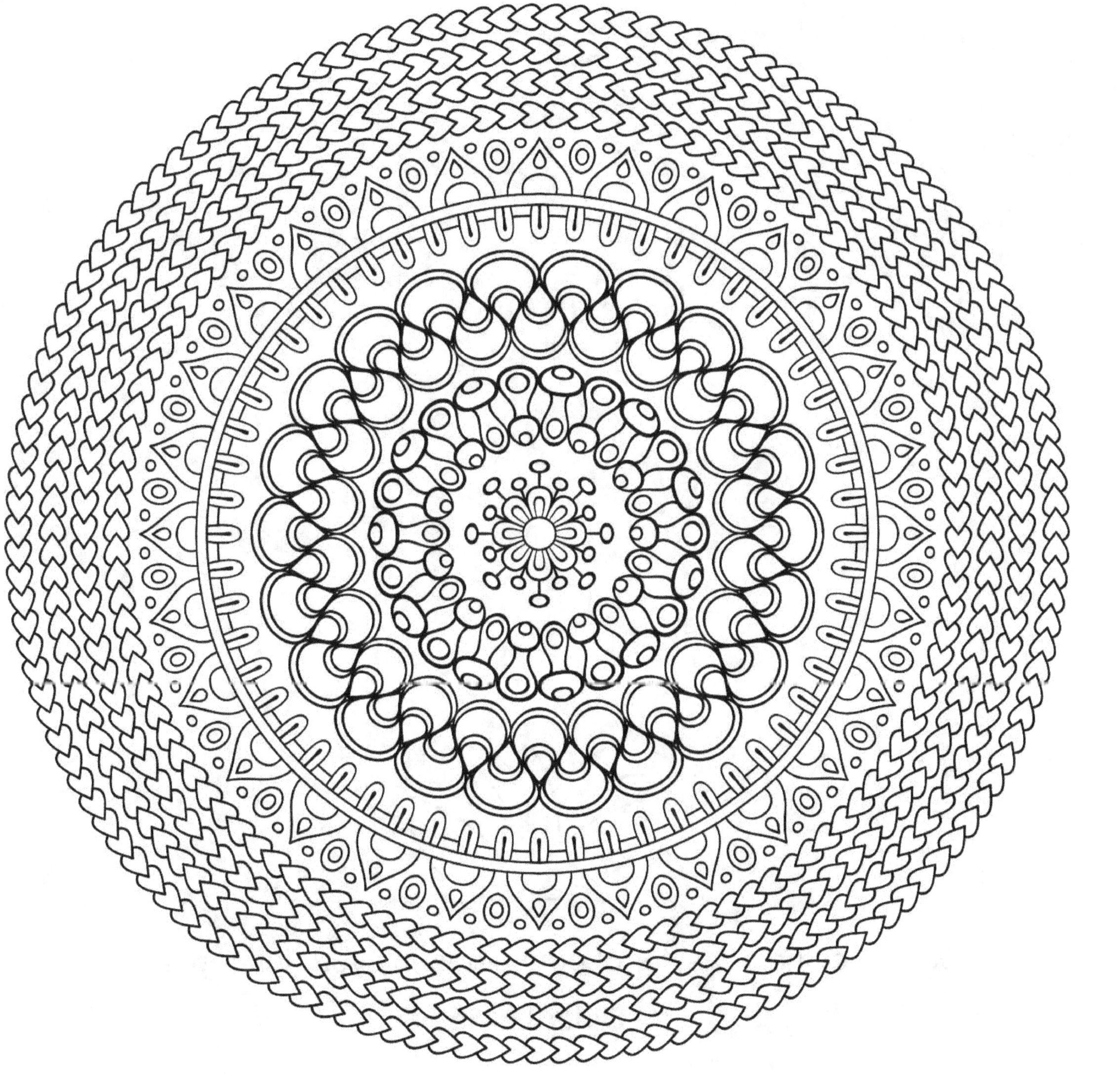

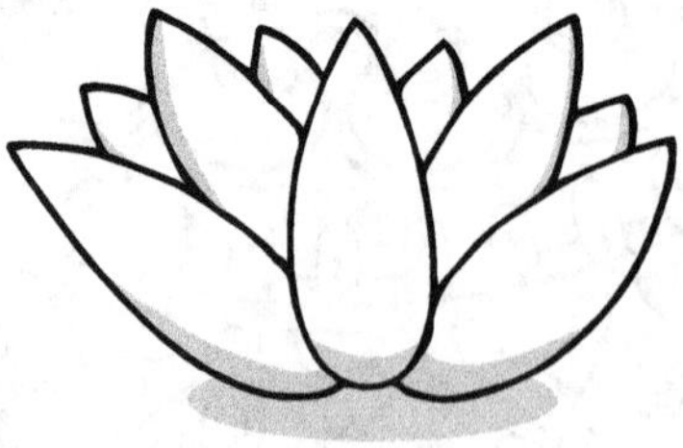

“Do not let the behavior of others destroy your inner peace.”

Dalai Lama

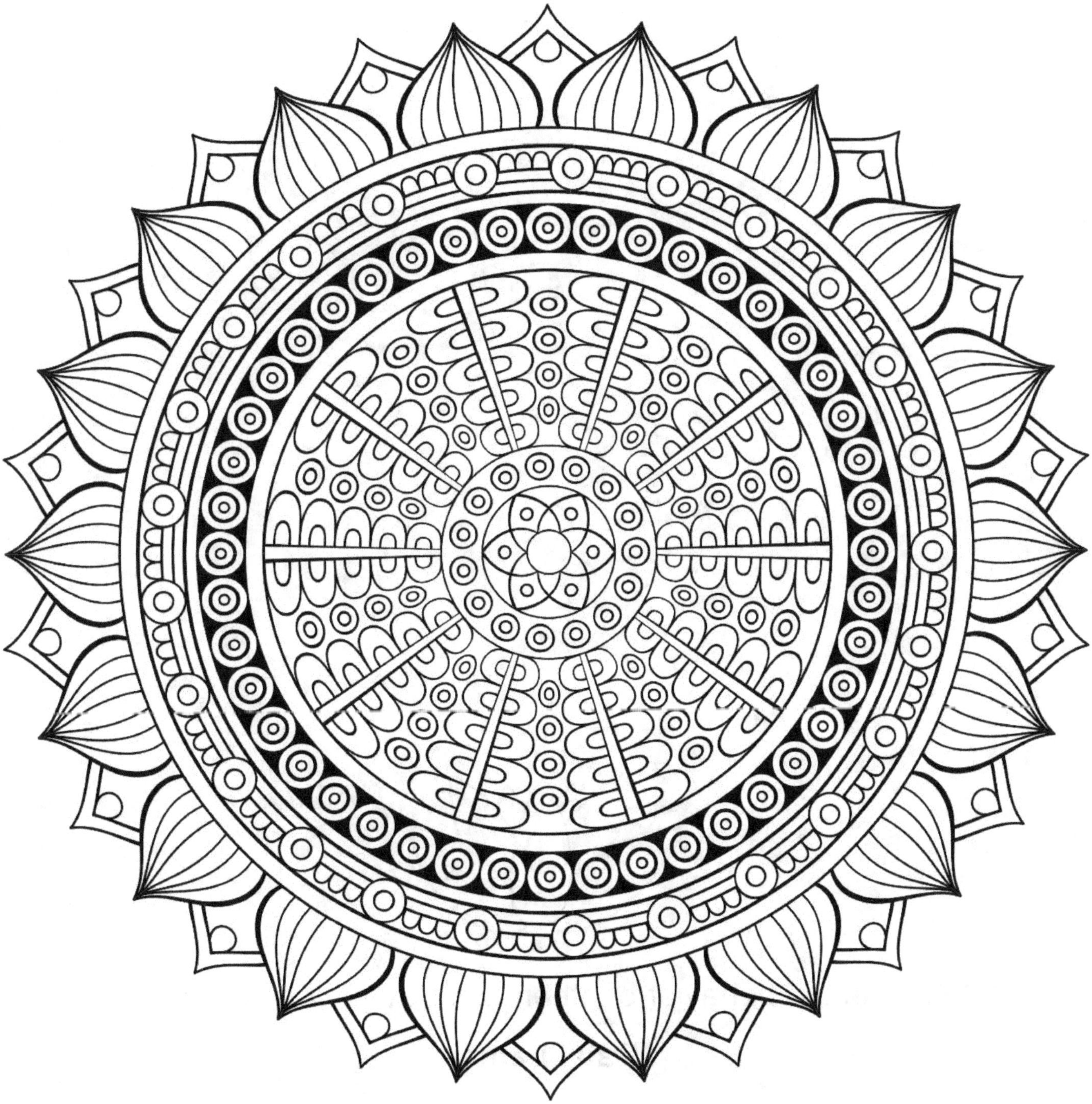

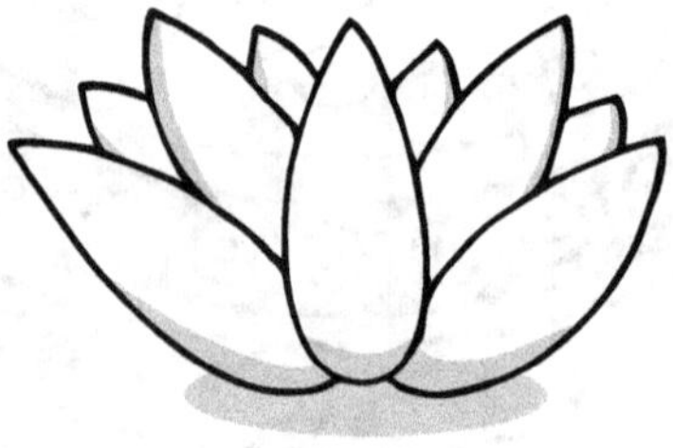

"Do not let the behavior of others destroy your inner peace."

Dalai Lama

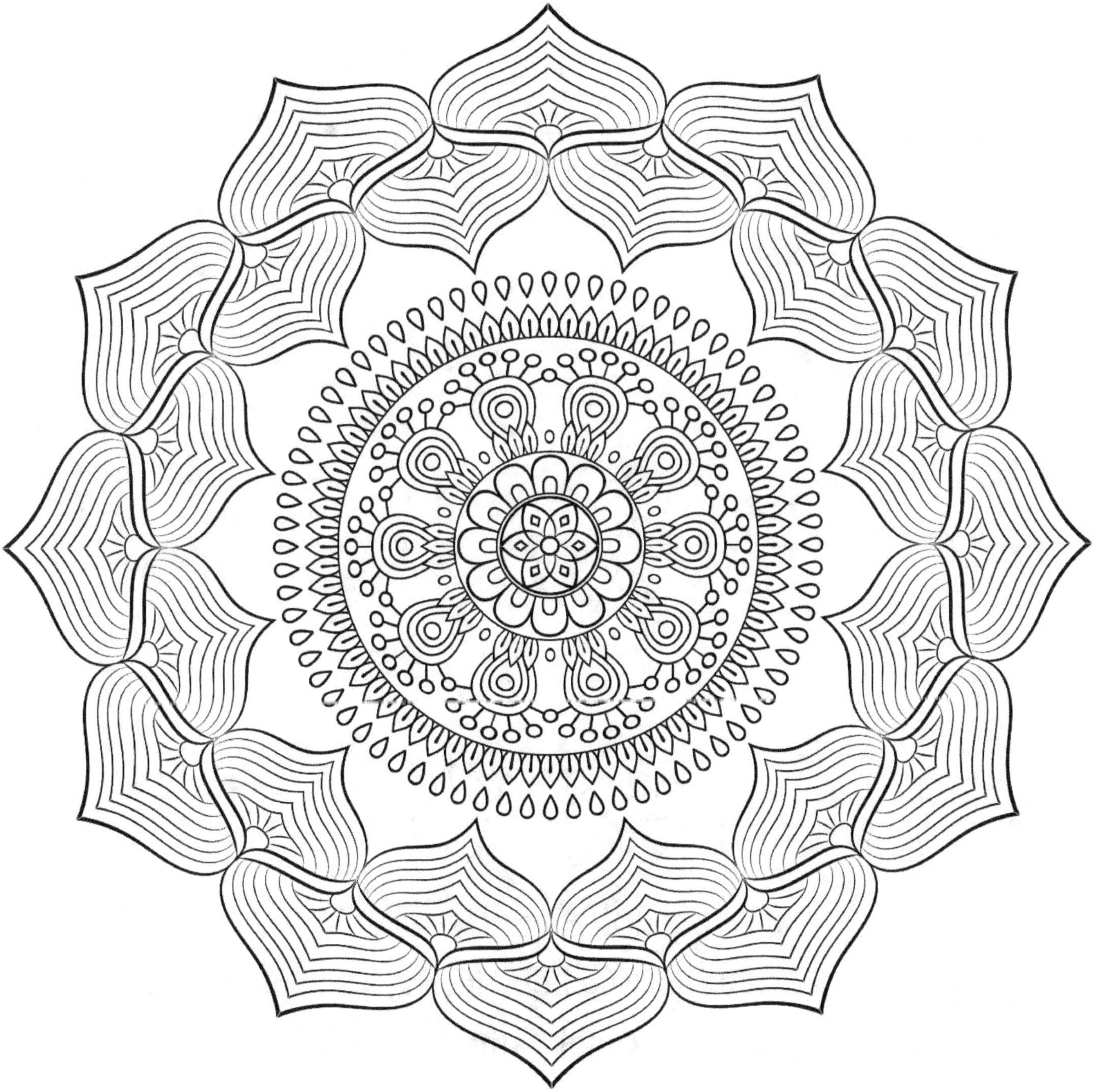

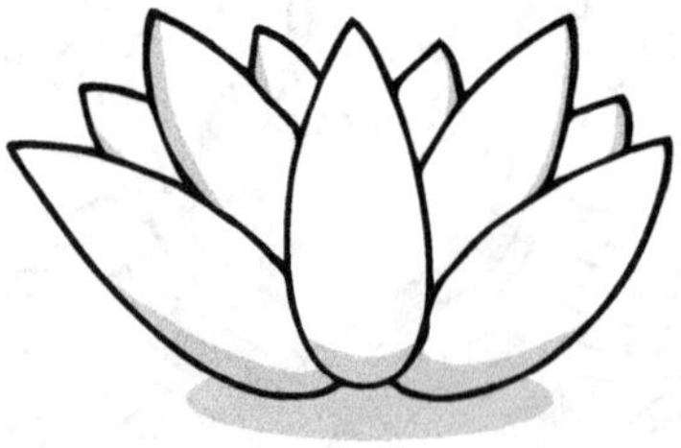

“Do not let the behavior of others destroy your inner peace.”

Dalai Lama

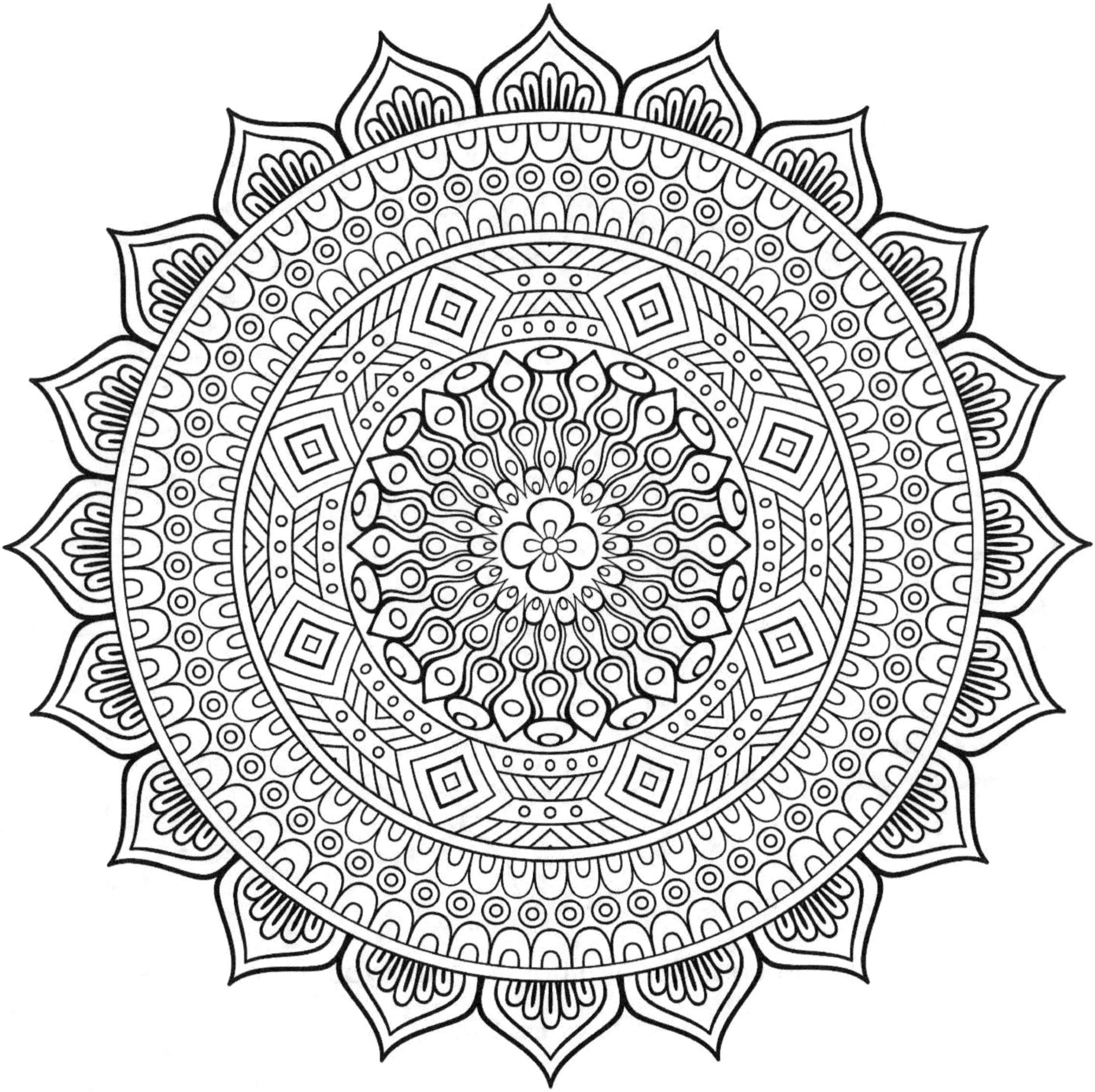

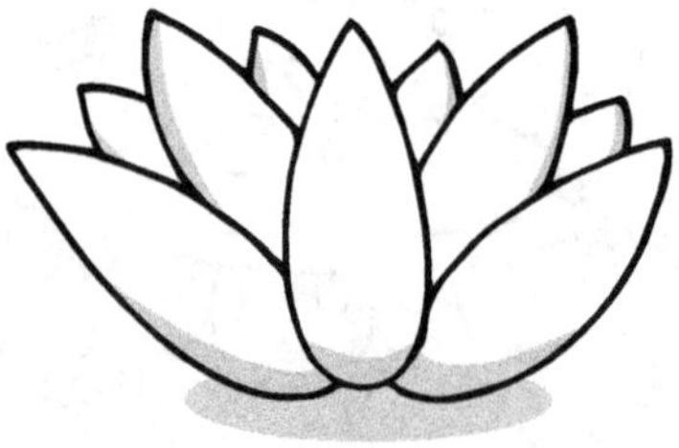

“Do not let the behavior of others destroy your inner peace.”

Dalai Lama

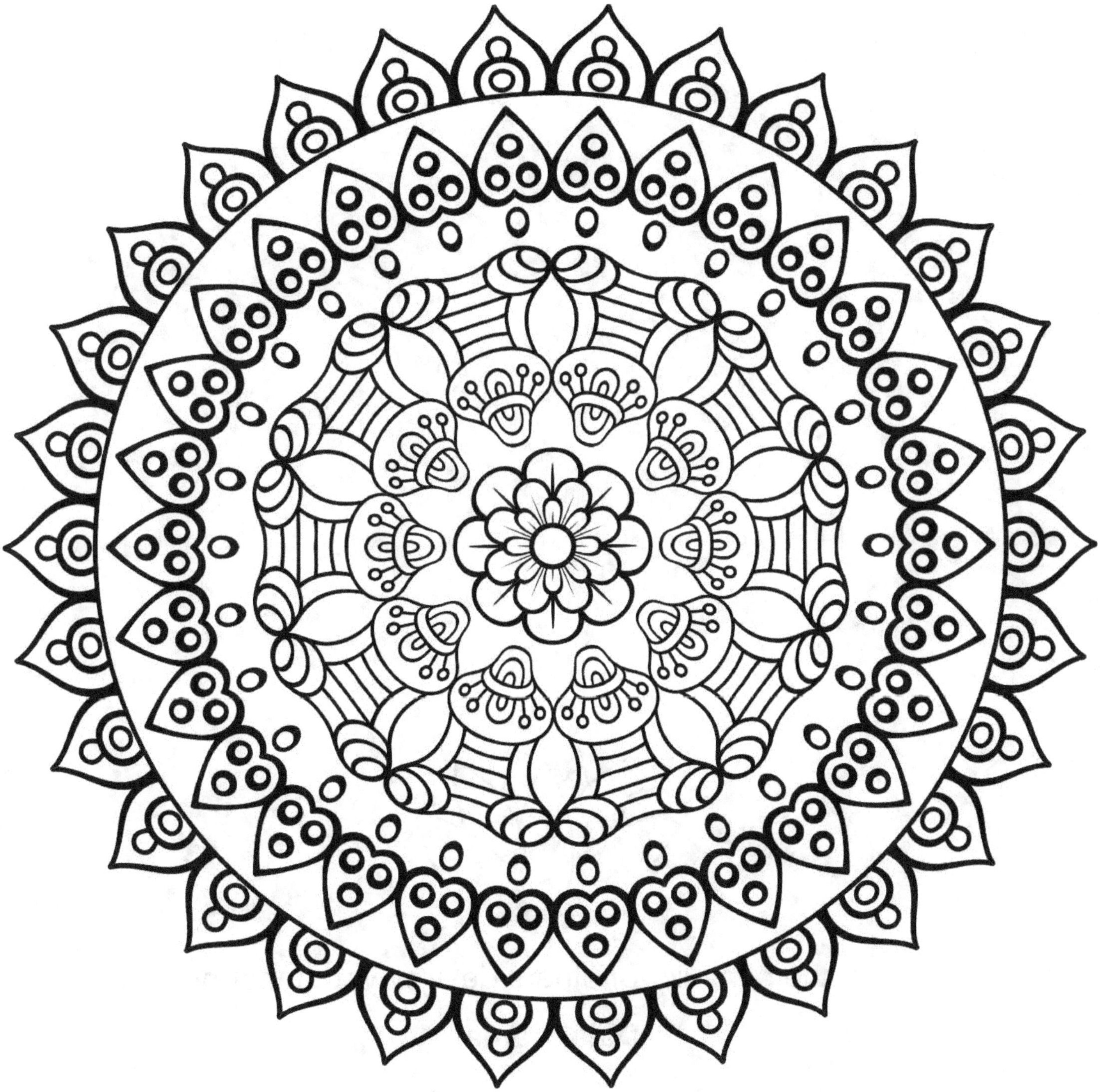

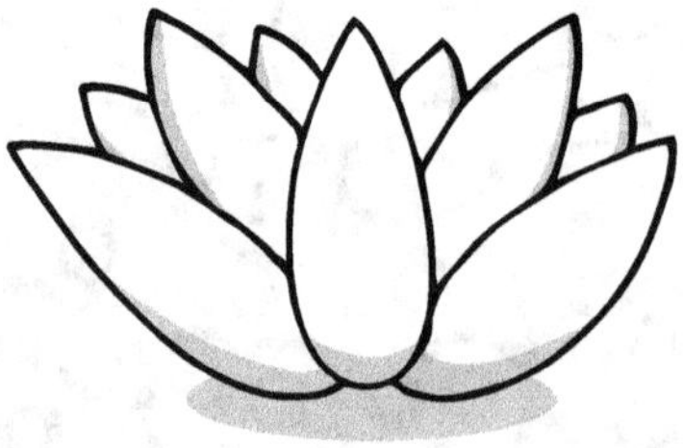

“Do not let the behavior of others destroy your inner peace.”

Dalai Lama

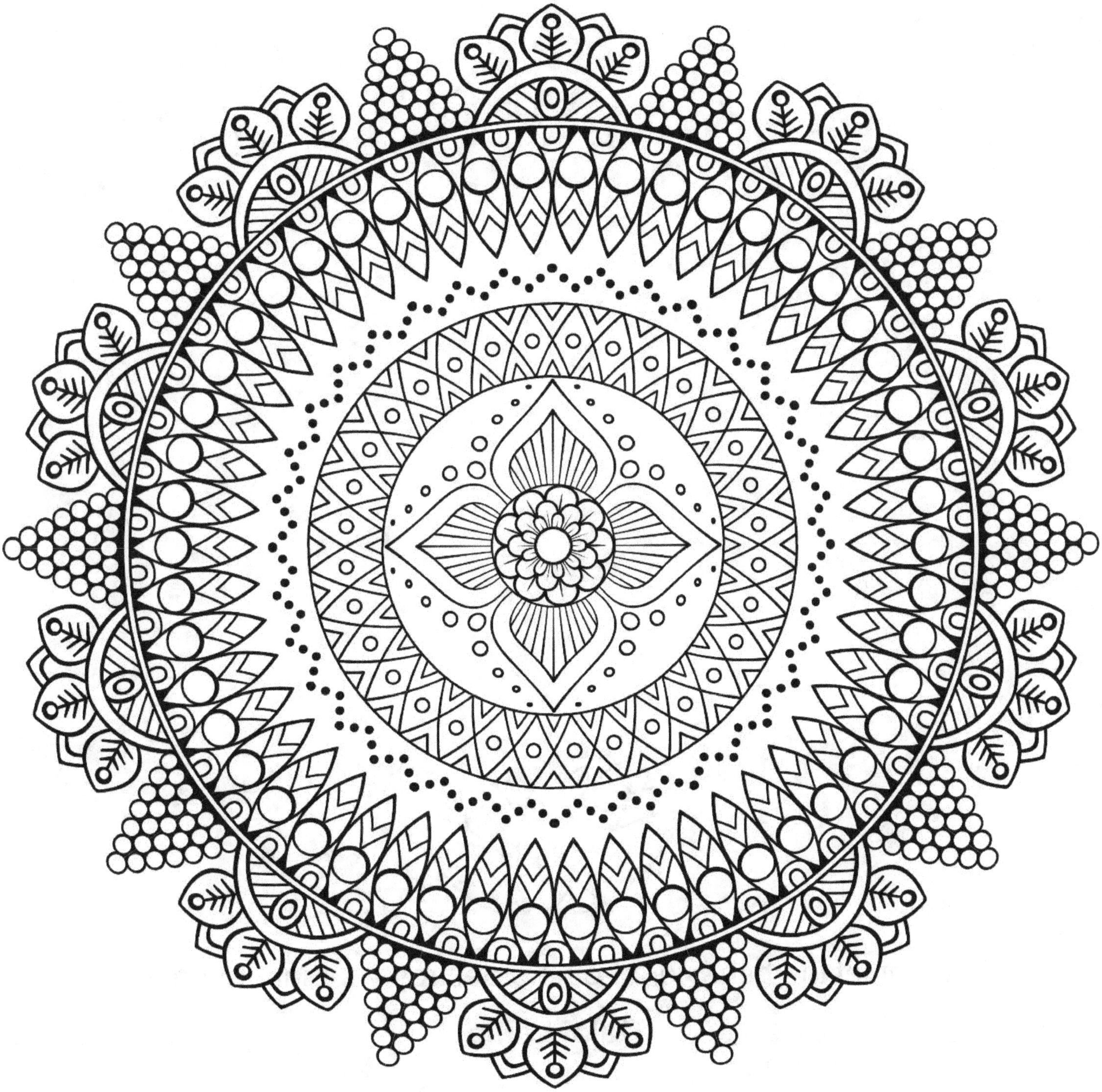

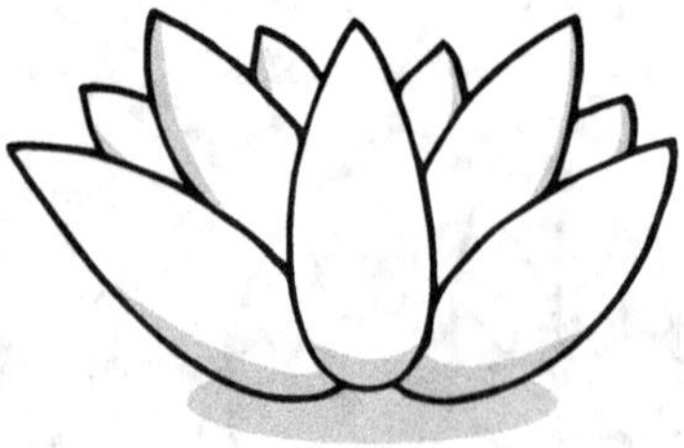

"Do not let the behavior of others destroy your inner peace."

Dalai Lama

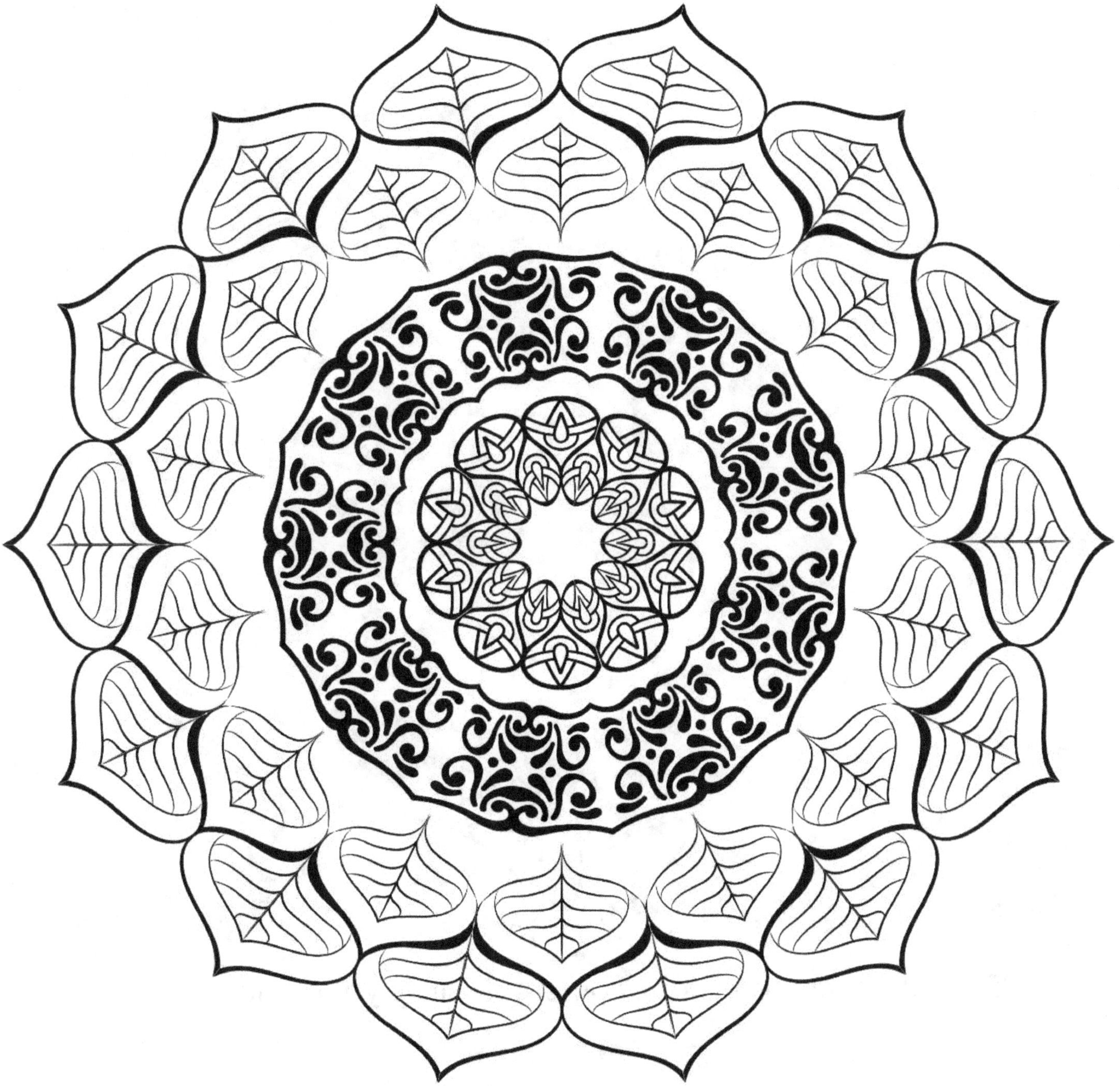

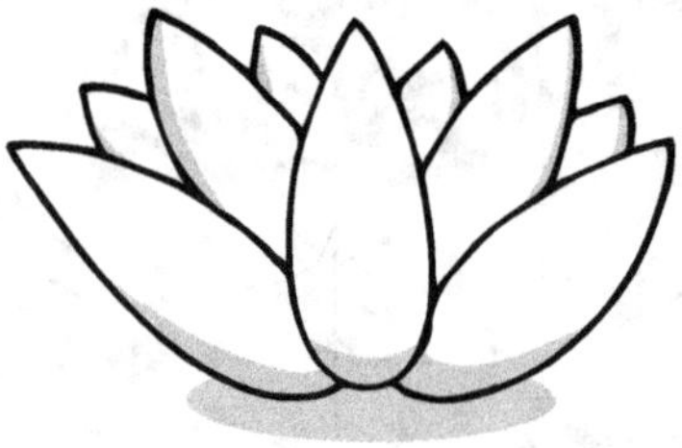

“Do not let the behavior of others destroy your inner peace.”

Dalai Lama

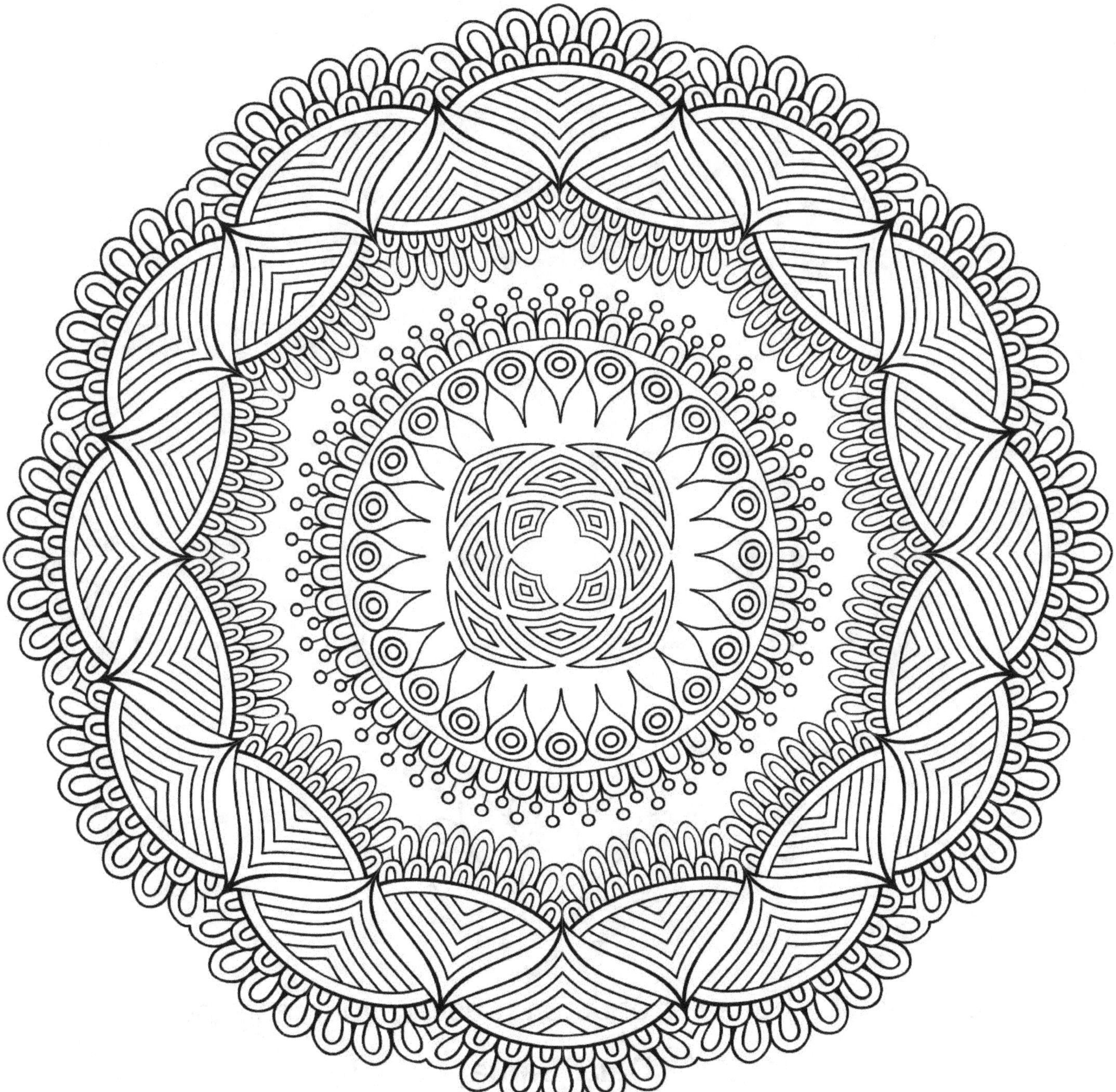

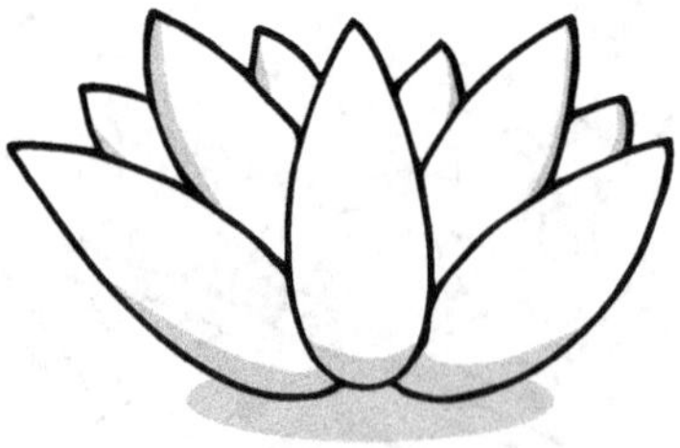

"Do not let the behavior of others destroy your inner peace."

Dalai Lama

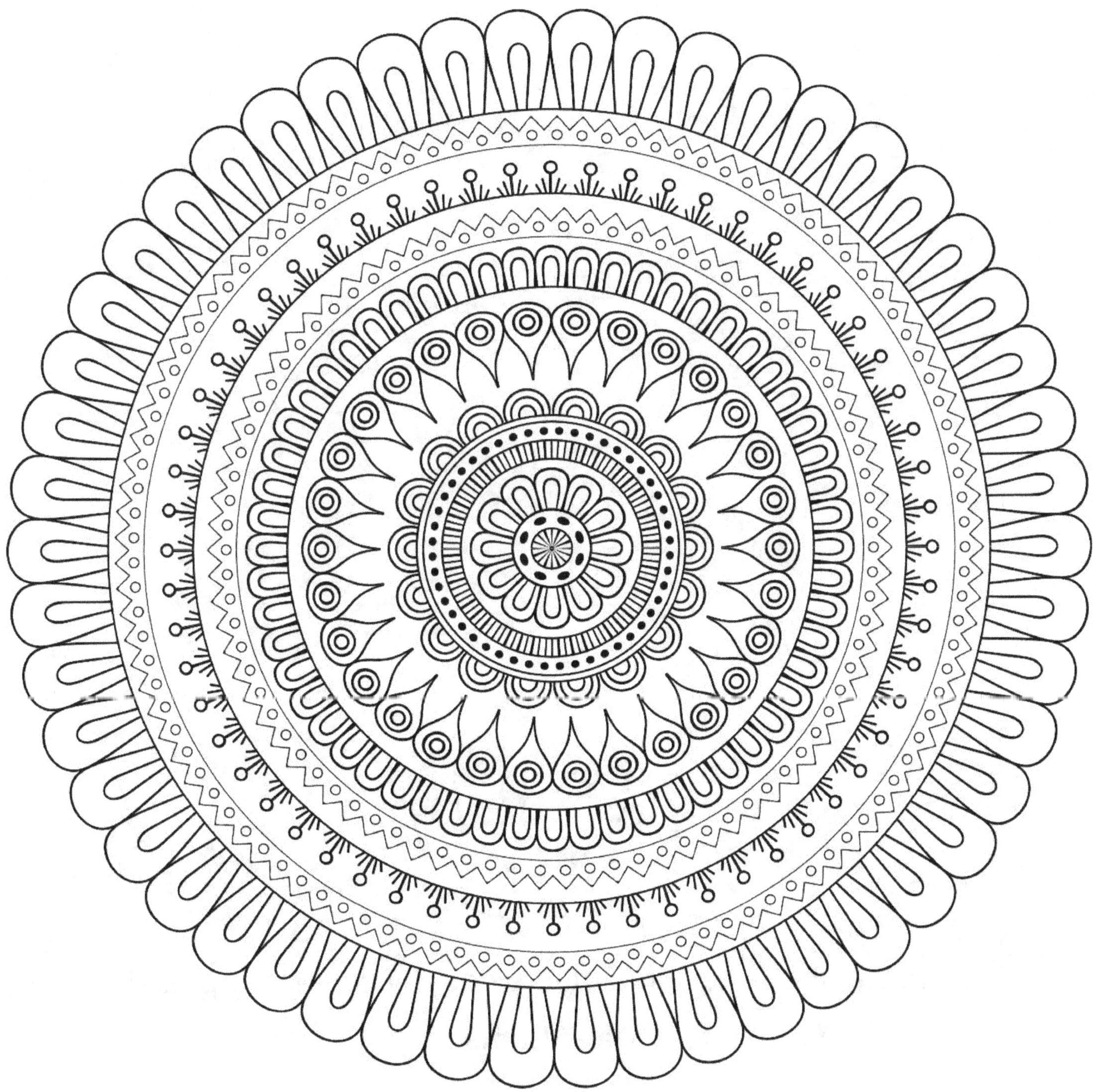

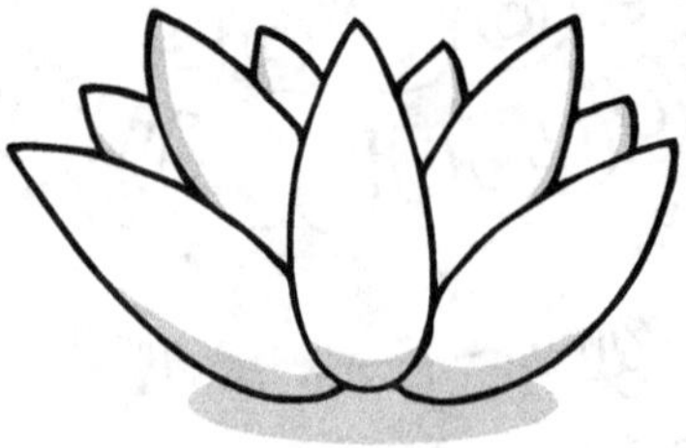

“Do not let the behavior of others destroy your inner peace.”

Dalai Lama

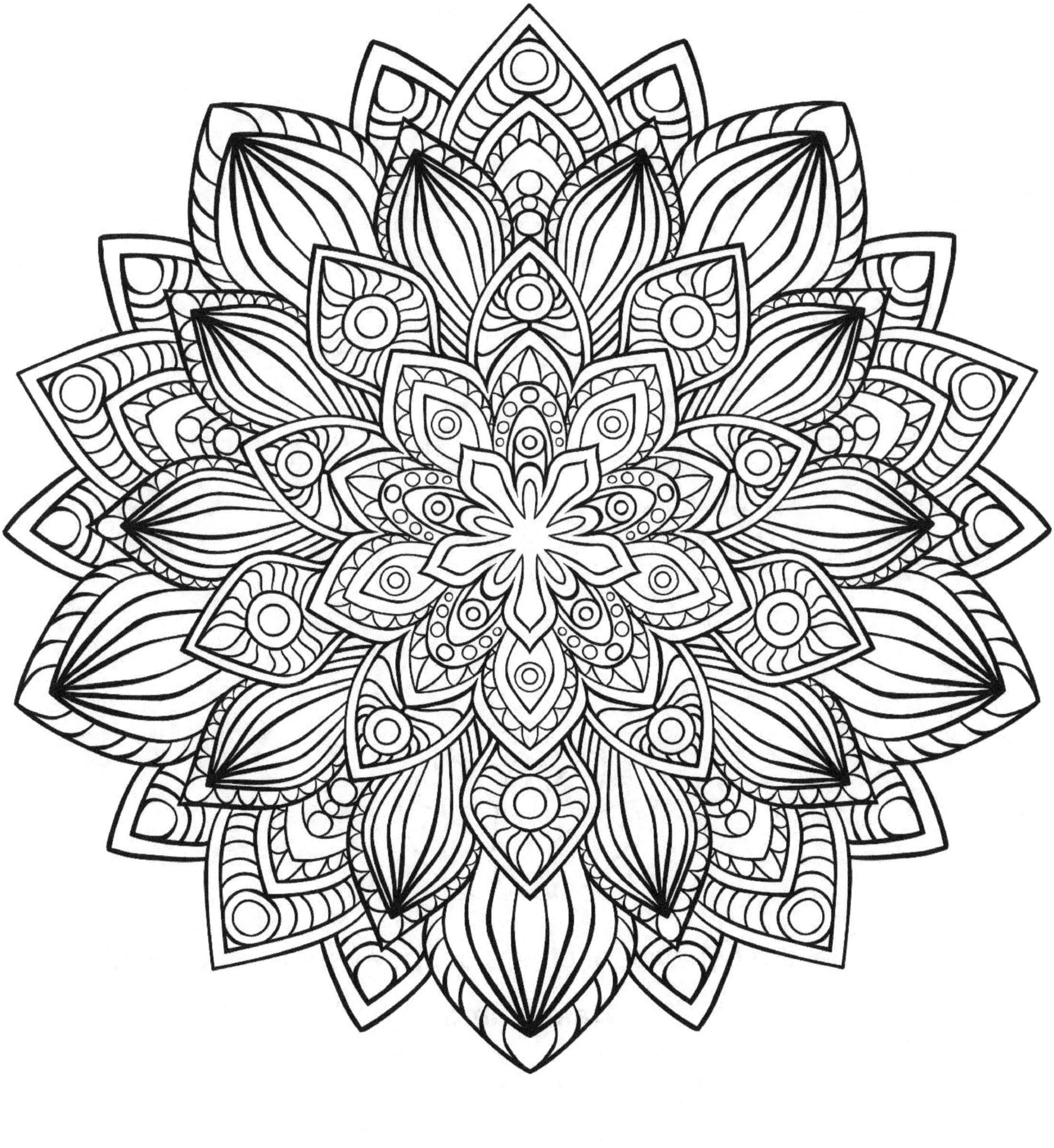

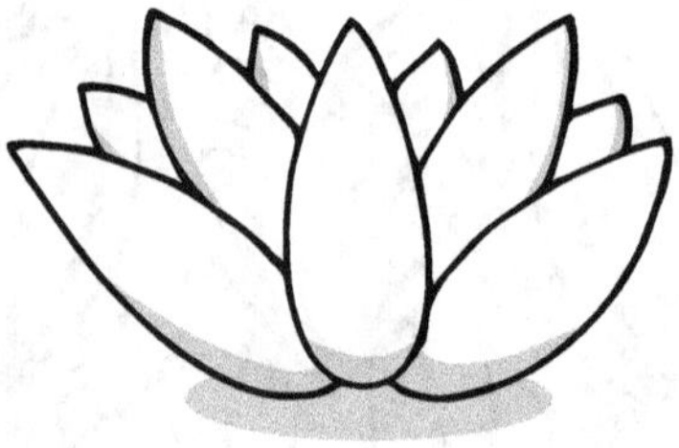

"Do not let the behavior of others destroy your inner peace."

Dalai Lama

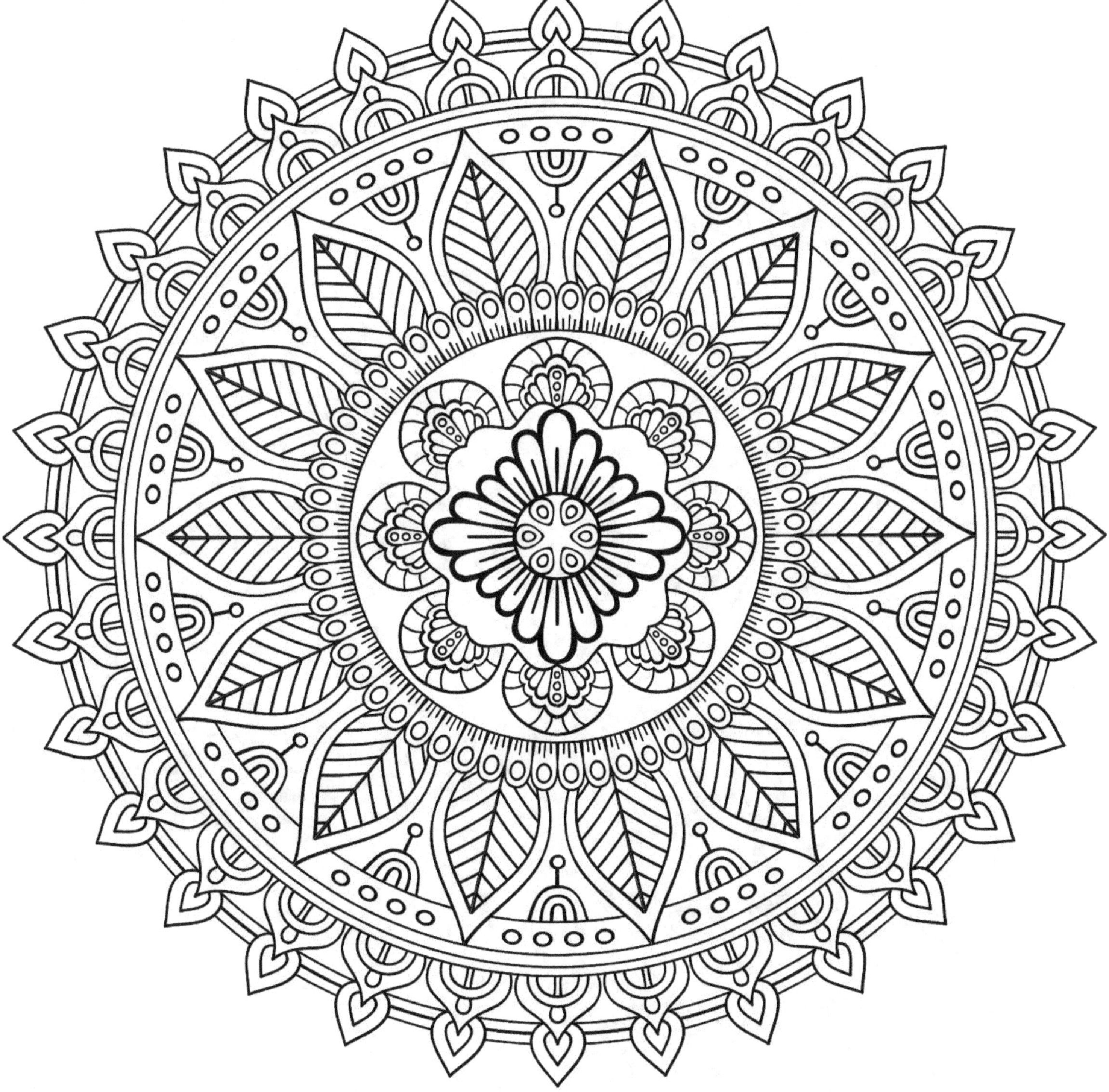

www.ingramcontent.com/pod-product-compliance
Lightning Source LLC
Chambersburg PA
CBHW080907220526
45466CB00011BA/3489
9781686046933